The God-man Living

Witness Lee

Living Stream Ministry
Anaheim, California

First Edition, 5,000 copies. July 1996.

ISBN 1-57593-316-0

Published by

Living Stream Ministry
1853 W. Ball Road, Anaheim, CA 92804 U.S.A.
P. O. Box 2121, Anaheim, CA 92814 U.S.A.

Printed in the United States of America

CONTENTS

PREFACE

This book is composed of messages given by Brother Witness Lee in Anaheim, California from February 21 through June 26, 1996.

THE GOD-MAN LIVING

MESSAGE ONE

BORN OF GOD THROUGH REGENERATION

Scripture Reading: John 3:16; Eph. 1:5, 9; Gen. 1:26; Prov. 20:27; Gen. 2:7; Eccl. 3:11; Gen. 2:9; 3:24; John 14:6; Heb. 10:19-20; John 1:1-5, 11-13; 3:6b, 3, 5

OUTLINE

I. God so loved the world that He gave them His only begotten Son, that they may receive Him by believing into Him to have the eternal life—the divine life—John 3:16.

II. His good pleasure is to be one with man and make man the same as He is in life and in nature but not in His Godhead—Eph. 1:5, 9.

III. He created man:

A. In His image and after His likeness—Gen. 1:26.

B. With a spirit (breath of life—spirit of man—Prov. 20:27) for man to receive and contain Him that man may live by Him as man's life (signified by the tree of life) and everything—Gen. 2:7.

C. Implanting in their heart eternity (a divinely implanted sense of a purpose working through the ages which nothing under the sun, but only God, can satisfy)—Eccl. 3:11.

D. Putting man in front of the tree of life (signifying God, the Creator of man, to be man's life)—Gen. 2:9.

IV. The way for man to contact God as the tree of life was closed due to man's fall by:

A. God's glory, signified by the cherubim.

B. God's holiness, signified by the burning flame.

    C. God's righteousness, signified by the slaying sword—Gen. 3:24.

V. This closed way was, in the New Testament, opened by the Lord through His death who fulfilled all the requirements of God's glory, holiness, and righteousness. Hence, now the crucified Christ becomes the reopened way for man to contact God as the tree of life—John 14:6; Heb. 10:19-20.

VI. The way the God-man is born of God through regeneration:

    A. In the creating Christ of all things as the Word of God is the divine life—John 1:1-4.

    B. This divine life in Christ is the light of men shining with the divine life over men in darkness—John 1:4-5.

    C. Whoever receives this shining light and believes into Christ as the Word of God who contains God's divine life will have the authority to become children of God—John 1:11-12.

    D. They are born not of blood (the physical life), nor of the will of the flesh (the will of fallen man after man became flesh), nor of the will of man (the will of the man created by God), but of God, who is the source of life and the fountain of life—John 1:13.

    E. All these children are God-men born of God.

    F. They are regenerated of God the Spirit to be spirits—gods (John 3:6b) belonging to the species of God to see and enter into the kingdom of God (John 3:3, 5).

In this series of messages we want to see the God-man living. This God-man living is the eight major items of Christ's organic saving: regeneration, shepherding, dispositional sanctification, renewing, transformation, building, conformation, and glorification. To touch the God-man living means to touch these eight major items. The commencement of the God-man living is our being born of God through regeneration. We need a particular beginning to have a certain kind of living. The living must have the birth as its beginning.

I. GOD LOVING THE WORLD
THAT THEY MAY HAVE ETERNAL LIFE

God so loved the world that He gave them His only begotten Son, that they may receive Him by believing into Him to have the eternal life—the divine life (John 3:16). John 3:16 says that God *so loved*. God loved the world so much, to such an extent, that He gave His only begotten Son to us. This was for the purpose that we may believe in Him and receive Him that we may have the eternal life. The eternal life is the goal of God's loving of us. Then we can be His children forming the church, issuing in the Body of Christ and consummating in the New Jerusalem. This conjoins God's love with the New Jerusalem. God's love is linked with the New Jerusalem, which is the ultimate consummation of God's love.

II. HIS GOOD PLEASURE

God's good pleasure is to be one with man and make man the same as He is in life and in nature but not in His Godhead (Eph. 1:5, 9). Ephesians 1:5 says that God predestinated us unto sonship according to the good pleasure of His will. *Unto sonship* means to make us sons. God predestinated us, marked us out, before the foundation of the world that we could be made His sons according to His good pleasure. If we would ask, "Father God, what is Your good pleasure?" He would say, "My good pleasure is to make Myself one with you and to make you My sons."

Ephesians 1:9 also speaks of God's good pleasure, which He purposed in Himself. God has some plan to fulfill, and this plan is to have the church as the Body of Christ which consummates in the New Jerusalem. We need the entire Bible to understand this one verse of the Bible in Ephesians. The good pleasure of God is to have us as His sons, and eventually, all these sons ultimately consummate the New Jerusalem. We should not forget these items—first, God loves us and second, He has a good pleasure. According to the revelation of the Bible, God's good pleasure is to have many sons and have all these many sons consummated as the New Jerusalem.

III. HIS CREATION OF MAN

In view of His good pleasure to have many sons consummated as the New Jerusalem, He created man in a special way.

A. In His Image and after His Likeness

According to Genesis 1:26 God created man in His image and after His likeness.

B. With a Spirit for Man to Receive and Contain Him

Furthermore, God created man with a spirit for man to receive and contain Him that man may live by Him as man's life (signified by the tree of life) and everything (Gen. 2:7). Man's human spirit is God's breath of life. The Hebrew word for *breath* in Genesis 2:7 is the same word for *spirit* in Proverbs 20:27, which says that the spirit of man is the lamp of the Lord.

C. Implanting Eternity in Their Heart

God created man in His image and with a human spirit for man to receive and contain Him. Ecclesiastes 3:11 also says that God put eternity in man's heart. The things in this universe are mainly of two categories: temporal things and eternal things. Paul in 2 Corinthians 4:18 said, "We do not regard the things which are seen but the things which are not seen; for the things which are seen are temporary, but the things which are not seen are eternal." This verse is the proper explanation of Solomon's word in Ecclesiastes 3:11.

The wise king said that God created everything beautiful in its own time and also put eternity in man's heart. This matches our human experience. Regardless of how rich or successful a person becomes, he still feels empty. Man has a deep desire for permanent things, and the only things which are permanent are the eternal things. The Amplified Bible says that eternity in man's heart is "a divinely implanted sense of a purpose working through the ages which nothing under the sun, but only God, can satisfy." We have a sense of a purpose which nothing can satisfy but God. Only God can satisfy the sense of purpose in our heart.

In God's creation of man there are three striking things: His image, our human spirit to receive Him, and a divinely implanted sense of a purpose in our hearts working through the ages which all things under the sun cannot satisfy—only God. The romance depicted in Song of Songs does not start from the Lord but from the seeker. A person becomes such a seeker because within him there is a sense of purpose to seek something eternal. Nothing can fulfill or satisfy this sense of purpose but God Himself, who is Christ. Many people would think that we are wasting our time, but actually we are redeeming the time. Those who pursue temporary things are wasting their time. They are busy for nothing. Anything they are busy for is temporary, not eternal. Only One in the whole universe is eternal, the eternal God.

D. Putting Man in Front of the Tree of Life

God created man in His image, with a human spirit, and with a sense of a purpose deeply implanted in man's heart. Then God put this man in front of the tree of life—signifying God, the Creator of man, to be man's life (Gen. 2:9).

IV. THE WAY FOR MAN TO CONTACT GOD AS THE TREE OF LIFE WAS CLOSED DUE TO MAN'S FALL

The way for man to contact God as the tree of life was closed due to man's fall by God's glory, signified by the cherubim, God's holiness, signified by the burning flame, and God's righteousness, signified by the slaying sword (Gen. 3:24). The slaying sword is for executing God's righteousness.

God's glory, God's holiness, and God's righteousness were the gatekeeper around the tree of life.

V. THE CRUCIFIED CHRIST
BECOMING THE REOPENED WAY FOR MAN
TO CONTACT GOD AS THE TREE OF LIFE

This closed way was, in the New Testament, opened by the Lord through His death who fulfilled all the requirements of God's glory, holiness, and righteousness. Hence, now the crucified Christ becomes the reopened way for man to contact God as the tree of life (John 14:6; Heb. 10:19-20). In John 14:6 the Lord said, "I am the way and the reality and the life." He became the way by being crucified. Hebrews 10 says that today a new way and a living way has been opened for us through His death. Christ with His death today is the reopened way for man to contact God as the tree of life.

VI. THE WAY THE GOD-MAN IS BORN OF GOD
THROUGH REGENERATION

A. In the Creating Christ
as the Word of God Is Life

Now we want to see the way the God-man is born of God through regeneration, the first item of the organic salvation of Christ. In the creating Christ of all things as the Word of God is the divine life (John 1:1-4). In John 1 there are five great events in the history of the universe: creation (v. 3), incarnation (v. 14), Christ being the Lamb of God for redemption (v. 29), Christ's becoming the life-giving Spirit for transformation (vv. 32, 42), and the building up of the house of God with Christ as the ladder bringing heaven to earth and joining earth to heaven (v. 51). Ultimately, the consummated New Jerusalem will be the very Bethel, the house of God. Christ as the ladder is for the traffic between heaven and earth. The angels of God, the serving ones, ascend and descend on this ladder to serve us. We are the house, the enjoyers.

In writing about Christ as the Word of God, speaking for God and revealing God, John chose these five events. In creation Christ spoke God. The creation speaks for God.

Psalm 19 says that the heavens declare the glory of God and that without a voice heard, the creation still speaks (vv. 1-4). Paul said in Romans 1:20 that God's eternal power and divine characteristics can be seen by man through God's creation. Eventually, millions of items of God's creation are praising God at the end of the Bible (Rev. 5:11-14). Creation is speaking God. That is the word of Christ speaking. Incarnation continues to speak and reveal God. John 1:29 says, "Behold, the Lamb of God, who takes away the sin of the world." This is also a big speaking. Then there is the transforming Spirit transforming the men of clay into stones for the building of Bethel, which will be the consummated New Jerusalem.

B. The Divine Life in Christ Being the Light of Men

These five great events in the history of the universe are the "trunk" of John 1. Out of this trunk a little branch springs up. This branch is that in this Word is life, and the life is the light that shines with the life (vv. 4-5). The divine life in Christ is the light of men shining with the divine life over men in darkness.

C. Having the Authority to Become Children of God

Whoever receives this shining light and believes into Christ as the Word of God who contains God's divine life will have the authority to become children of God (vv. 11-12).

D. Born of God

These ones are born not of blood (the physical life), nor of the will of the flesh (the will of fallen man after man became flesh), nor of the will of man (the will of the man created by God), but of God, who is the source of life and the fountain of life (v. 13). God is the source of life. He is also the fountain of life that flows. In John's writings he describes God as the flowing One. Eventually, the Triune God flows out as the river of the water of life, and this flow reaches all the twelve gates of the New Jerusalem on the four sides to satisfy and nourish the entire city (Rev. 22:1). God as the fountain flows out as the spring in John 4:14.

The Lord gives us the water of life which becomes in us a spring of water gushing up into eternal life.

Not many Christians have paid full attention to regeneration as they should. Our being born of our parents was our first birth. Then one day we received Christ because of His light, and we were regenerated. We had another birth. But I would ask: Of these two births which one receives more of our attention—the first birth of our parents or the second birth of God? We should not pay attention to our first birth. We should remember only one birth, our regeneration. Day by day, we should not forget that we are children of God, born not of blood, nor of the will of the flesh, nor of the will of man, but of God. Today we believers in Christ know who our Father is. We respect our second birth, the birth in which we were born of the very God.

E. The Children of God Being God-men

The children of God are God-men born of God.

F. Belonging to the Species of God

We are regenerated of God the Spirit to be spirits—gods (John 3:6b) belonging to the species of God to see and enter into the kingdom of God (vv. 3, 5). John 1 tells us how we received the authority to be the children of God. Then John 3 speaks of regeneration again. Verse 6 says, "That which is born of the flesh is flesh, and that which is born of the Spirit is spirit." We are the flesh and born of the flesh in our natural life. But we were born of God the Spirit to be spirits, gods. That which is born of a cow is a cow. That which is born of a horse is a horse. We are born of the Spirit, and the Spirit is God. John 4:24 tells us clearly that God is Spirit. Because we are born of God the Spirit, we must be gods in life and in nature but not in the Godhead. If we do not believe that we who are born of God are gods, then what are we? That which is born of the Spirit is spirit.

Our second birth caused us to enter into the kingdom of God to become the species of God. The animals and plants have their particular species. We are born of God, so we are gods belonging to the species of God. We should always remember that we are God-men belonging to the species of God. A God-man does not quarrel with others. This is an intrinsic-study of the Word of God.

Regeneration is the first step of Christ's organic salvation. The washing of regeneration purges away all the things of the old nature of our old man (Titus 3:5). This washing is an organic saving. Without regeneration's washing, there would be layers of the old creation in our being. Perhaps some would feel that they are not of the species of God, but of the "species" of the Americans. This species should be washed away. We need to see that regeneration as the first step of Christ's organic saving is to wash away the layers of the old creation of our old nature.

We must not forget that we are God-men belonging to God's species. As God-men born of God and belonging to God's species, we cannot speak to our spouse in a loose way. A husband must be a God-man, living as a God-man. To be merely a good man is far away from God's good pleasure. We need to see that we are God-men, born of God and belonging to God's species. This is the beginning of the God-man living.

God loves you. God has a good pleasure to make you the same as He is. He is God, so you must be God also. A God-man living is God living. This kind of teaching is much higher than the teaching concerning how to be holy or victorious. In my early days as a believer, I saw many books on how to live the Christian life, but these books did not really reveal the way. How can you be holy? You can be holy by living a God-man life. How can you be victorious? It is only by living a God-man life. Never forget that you are a God-man, born of God and belonging to God's species.

THE GOD-MAN LIVING

MESSAGE TWO

UNDER THE ORGANIC FEEDING AND SHEPHERDING OF CHRIST AS THE GOOD SHEPHERD

Scripture Reading: John 11:25; 14:6; 10:10b-11, 14, 16; 21:15-17; Eph. 4:11-13; 1 Pet. 5:4; Heb. 13:20; 1 Pet. 2:25, 2; 1 Cor. 3:2; Heb. 5:13-14; 1 Thes. 2:7; Eph. 5:29; Col. 1:28; Eph. 6:17; 1 Cor. 12:11; Eph. 4:4; 1 Pet. 5:2; Acts 20:28

OUTLINE

  I. The Gospel of John, as the gospel of life, unveils to us that Christ is not only life (11:25; 14:6) for Him to be life to us that through Him we may be regenerated by God, but also a good Shepherd (10:10b-11, 14, 16) who feeds and shepherds us as His flock.

 II. After their spiritual birth, as newborn babes, the believers need the feeding and the shepherding of Christ, as He charged Peter, His first apostle, to take care of the believers as His lambs and sheep by feeding and shepherding them—John 21:15-17.

III. In the church life Christ as the Head distributes His gifts to the mature ones, among whom are the shepherds, for the perfecting of the saints and the building up of the Body of Christ—Eph. 4:11-12.

IV. Christ, who is the believers' Redeemer, Savior, and life, becomes the Chief Shepherd (1 Pet. 5:4) and the great Shepherd (Heb. 13:20), who shepherds His believers as their Overseer (1 Pet. 2:25).

  V. Shepherding includes feeding, especially in taking care of the newborn ones, and for the feeding of the newborn ones, milk is the best (1 Pet. 2:2; 1 Cor. 3:2a; Heb. 5:13); the apostle Paul likened himself to such a nursing mother (1 Thes. 2:7).

VI. Both the feeding and the shepherding are for the God-men's growth in the divine life of God for their daily salvation—1 Pet. 2:2b.

VII. The shepherds' feeding is not only for the growth unto the believers' daily salvation but also unto their maturity in the divine life which is needed for the God-men to be built up in the Body of Christ—Heb. 5:14; Eph. 4:12-13.

VIII. Christ as the Head of the Body nourishes and cherishes us (Eph. 5:29). Christ's shepherding includes nourishing and cherishing; nourishing is to feed us, and cherishing is to comfort us, to soothe us, to nurture us with tender love, and to foster us with tender care. All of this is to help us grow in the divine life that we may be full-grown and matured in it (Col. 1:28; Eph. 4:13).

IX. Christ's feeding is for the believers' growth in the divine life, and the God-men's growth in the divine life is for the manifestation of their functions in the Body of Christ.

X. The believers' growth in the divine life is by feeding on the word of God, which is also the Spirit of God (Eph. 6:17), and the manifestation of the believers' functions in the Body of Christ is also by the Spirit (1 Cor. 12:11); hence, the feeding of Christ is related eventually to the Spirit who is altogether for the Body of Christ (Eph. 4:4) to consummate the ultimate goal of God's eternal economy.

XI. Such feeding and shepherding of Christ should be the responsibility of the elders for the churches (1 Pet. 5:2; Acts 20:28) and the great part of the function of our today's vital groups.

In the previous message we pointed out that even from eternity God fell in love with man. God's good pleasure is to be one with man, to make Himself a man, and to make man Himself in life and in nature but not in the Godhead. In order to accomplish His good pleasure, God created three important things for man. First, He created man in His image, making man His xerox copy; second, He created man with a human spirit; and third, He put eternity in man's heart. The word for *eternity* may also be translated "the ages." The Amplified Bible gives a marvelous translation of this word in Ecclesiastes 3:11 by saying that eternity in man's heart indicates a divinely implanted sense of a purpose working through the ages which nothing under the sun, but only God, can satisfy.

After His creation of man, God put man in front of the tree of life, but the way to the tree of life was closed due to man's fall. The crucified Christ later became the reopened way for man to contact God as the tree of life. When man receives the life of God, he is regenerated. Regeneration is to bring forth the children of God. Shepherding is to take care of the children by feeding them. After shepherding comes dispositional sanctification and renewing, transformation and building, and conformation unto the image of the firstborn Son of God and glorification. These are the eight items of God's organic salvation.

God's organic salvation is His salvation by His life. The line of the inner life started with Madame Guyon and other mystics. William Law improved these mystical writings, and later Andrew Murray used William Law's writings. Mrs. Penn-Lewis, who received help from Andrew Murray's writings, went on to see the subjective death of Christ. Following her, T. Austin-Sparks saw the principles of life in resurrection. But all of these saints in the line of the inner life never considered the Lord's shepherding a part of the Lord's organic salvation.

The shepherding work is to feed. Feeding is the business of a nursing mother. After parents beget children, they have to feed them so that they can live. Feeding is a part of God's organic salvation. In the God-man living we are firstly born of God through regeneration. Then we are under the organic feeding and shepherding of Christ as the good Shepherd. After our birth we need feeding to progress in life.

Shepherding and feeding are a part of the God-man living. The God-men are just the believers. In this message I use *believers* and *God-men* interchangeably. In the New Testament we cannot find the term *God-men,* but a synonym for *God-men* is *the children of God. (The children of God* is used ten times in the New Testament.) John 1:12 says, "But as many as received Him, to them He gave the authority to become children of God, to those who believe into His name." Romans 8:16 says, "The Spirit Himself witnesses with our spirit that we are children of God." The children of God are the God-men.

We saw in message one that the children of God belong to the species of God. A species is a kingdom. There are the plant kingdom, the animal kingdom, the human kingdom, and the God kingdom. John 3 says that when we are born of God, we see and enter into the kingdom of God (vv. 3, 5). The word *kingdom* here refers to the organic realm, the species, not to the governmental realm. The Lord told Nicodemus that unless he was regenerated he would not be able to see, or understand, the kingdom of God. Who can understand the kingdom of lions if he is not a lion? If you are born of a lion to be a small lion, right away you see, understand, the kingdom of lions. To see is to intrinsically understand.

Once we are born into the kingdom of God to be the children of God, the God-men, we need the feeding. We should not think that every God-man is full-grown. The God-men begin their spiritual lives as babes. But regardless of our spiritual maturity, we all need the organic feeding and shepherding of Christ.

I. CHRIST BEING THE GOOD SHEPHERD

The Gospel of John, as the Gospel of life, unveils to us that Christ is not only life (11:25; 14:6) for Him to be life to us that through Him we may be regenerated by God, but also a good Shepherd (10:10b-11, 14, 16) who feeds and shepherds us as His flock. In Song of Songs the Lord instructs His lover to go to the place where He pastures His sheep by following the footsteps of His flock (1:7-8). Later, He also pastures His flock among the lilies, that is, among those who seek the Lord and live a life of trusting in God with a pure heart (2:16; 6:3).

II. THE CHILDREN OF GOD NEEDING THE FEEDING AND SHEPHERDING OF CHRIST

After their spiritual birth, as newborn babes, the children of God need the feeding and the shepherding of Christ, as He charged Peter, His first apostle, to take care of the believers as His lambs and sheep by feeding and shepherding them (John 21:15-17). John 21 is an appendix to the Gospel of John. In this appendix Christ came in resurrection to the apostles to charge Peter to feed the Lord's lambs and to shepherd His sheep.

III. THE SHEPHERDS FOR THE PERFECTING OF THE SAINTS

In the church life Christ as the Head distributes His gifts to the mature ones, among whom are the shepherds, for the perfecting of the saints and the building up of the Body of Christ (Eph. 4:11-12). We all need some shepherds to come to perfect us. This is needed for the vital groups. Vital groups must be groups of God-men.

IV. CHRIST BEING THE CHIEF SHEPHERD AND THE GREAT SHEPHERD

Christ, who is the believers' Redeemer, Savior, and life, becomes the Chief Shepherd (1 Pet. 5:4) and the great Shepherd (Heb. 13:20), who shepherds His believers as their Overseer (1 Pet. 2:25). *The Chief Shepherd* is Peter's word; *the great Shepherd* is Paul's word. All of God's believers should be under this one Shepherd, who cares for the believers as their Overseer. The churches are so weak because they are missing the vital groups with Christ as the Chief Shepherd and Overseer. I hope that in these next few years we will practice anew the vital groups with the elements of feeding and shepherding. If we do not know how to feed and shepherd others, we cannot have the vital groups.

V. SHEPHERDING INCLUDING FEEDING

Shepherding includes feeding, especially in taking care of the newborn ones, and for the feeding of the newborn ones, milk is the best (1 Pet. 2:2; 1 Cor. 3:2a; Heb. 5:13); the apostle Paul likened himself to such a nursing mother (1 Thes. 2:7).

VI. FOR THE GOD-MEN'S GROWTH IN THE DIVINE LIFE

Both the feeding and the shepherding are for the God-men's growth in the divine life of God for their daily salvation (1 Pet. 2:2b). We need God's organic salvation to be our daily salvation. First Peter 2:2 says that the newborn babes desire the milk from God's word that they may grow unto salvation, the daily salvation. We need to be saved from such things as losing our temper, criticizing others, mistreating others, and even lying. We need an everyday salvation from such sinful practices. We can be saved by being fed with the milk of the word.

Even in such a great and deep book like Ephesians, Paul said that the one who steals should steal no more (4:28). Such a high and deep book still has such a lower charge. If there were a stealer among us, perhaps we would feel that he is not saved. But Paul indicated that such saved ones are in need of a daily salvation. They need to have Ephesians 4:28 for their morning watch: "He who steals should steal no more."

Paul also spoke in Ephesians about honoring our parents (6:1-3). All the young people among us need this word. Also, regardless of how old a person becomes, he should still honor his parents. A brother talks to his own children in one way, but to his parents in another way. The way in which we speak to our parents must be in an honoring way. In today's age some children address their parents by their first name. This is not an honoring or respectful way to speak to one's parents. For such daily-life sins, we need a daily salvation by feeding on the milk of the word. Then we can grow unto daily salvation.

VII. THE SHEPHERDS' FEEDING BEING FOR THE BELIEVERS' MATURITY IN THE DIVINE LIFE

The shepherds' feeding is not only for the growth unto the believers' daily salvation but also unto their maturity in the divine life which is needed for the God-men to be built up in the Body of Christ (Heb. 5:14; Eph. 4:12-13). After observing the saints for so many years, I wonder how the Body of Christ could be built up. Some elders are too strong, while others are too weak. Both are wrong. If an elder is either too strong or too weak, he is disqualified from the eldership. Only those who are mild, not so strong and not so weak, are qualified to be elders. Some brothers are very good, but they do not like to talk to people. Because they know the Lord and the truth, they should be strong members of the vital groups, but they hardly ever speak. Some are so strong among us and others are so weak. As a result, there is no building. There is no building because we do not live the life of a God-man. The God-man living will make us fit to be built in the Body of Christ. This living is the issue of our feeding on the milk of the word so that we can grow in our daily life unto salvation.

VIII. NOURISHING AND CHERISHING

Christ as the Head of the Body nourishes and cherishes us (Eph. 5:29). Christ's shepherding includes nourishing and cherishing; nourishing is to feed us, and cherishing is to comfort us, to soothe us, to nurture us with tender love, and to foster us with tender care. All of this is to help us grow in the divine life that we may be full-grown and matured in it (Col. 1:28; Eph. 4:13). Cherishing people makes them happy. In the church life, sometimes we have to make people happy in the Lord.

IX. THE MANIFESTATION OF THE FUNCTIONS IN THE BODY OF CHRIST

Christ's feeding is for the believers' growth in the divine life, and the God-men's growth in the divine life is for the manifestation of their functions in the Body of Christ.

X. THE FEEDING OF CHRIST BEING RELATED TO THE SPIRIT, WHO IS ALTOGETHER FOR THE BODY OF CHRIST

The believers' growth in the divine life is by feeding on the word of God, which is also the Spirit of God (Eph. 6:17), and the manifestation of the believers' functions in the Body of Christ is also by the Spirit (1 Cor. 12:11); hence, the feeding of Christ is related eventually to the Spirit who is altogether for the Body of Christ (Eph. 4:4) to consummate the ultimate goal of God's eternal economy. Whatever we do in shepherding and feeding others is related to the Spirit. All of the God-man's living is related to the Spirit, so we must be men of the Spirit. Only a man of the Spirit can have a proper God-man living.

XI. THE RESPONSIBILITY OF THE ELDERS AND THE GREAT PART OF THE FUNCTION OF THE VITAL GROUPS

Such feeding and shepherding of Christ should be the responsibility of the elders for the churches (1 Pet. 5:2; Acts 20:28) and the great part of the function of our today's vital groups. If someone does not know how to feed and shepherd others, he is not qualified to be an elder. The responsibility of an elder is to feed and to shepherd the saints, and the greater part of the function of today's vital groups is also feeding and shepherding. Feeding and shepherding takes time and requires patience. We must have patience with endurance to practice the vital groups. We should not expect quick fruit. Quick fruit comes and goes. We have to spend our time to feed and shepherd others. This is what the Lord is doing with us.

Even today, as an old follower of Christ, I need His feeding and shepherding. I realize that very few people understand my suffering related to my age. The only one who knows my suffering is Christ, so I need Him to shepherd and feed me. He is my Chief Shepherd and great Shepherd. All of us need to be under the organic feeding and shepherding of Christ and be one with Him to feed and shepherd others.

THE GOD-MAN LIVING

MESSAGE THREE

THE FIRST GOD-MAN'S LIVING
FROM THE MANGER TO THE CROSS

(1)

Scripture Reading: Luke 2:7-16; Matt. 2:1-23; Luke 2:21-24;
Col. 2:11; Luke 2:25, 34-35, 40, 49, 52; 3:23; Isa. 53:2-3; 52:14;
Heb. 4:15b; 2:18; Num. 4:3

OUTLINE

I. In His infancy:
   A. Lying in a manger—Luke 2:7-16.
   B. Fleeing from His opposers:
      1. From the land of Israel to Egypt—Matt. 2:1-15.
      2. From Egypt back to the land of Israel—Matt. 2:16-21.
      3. From Bethlehem to Galilee and settled in Nazareth—Matt. 2:22-23.

II. In His youth:
   A. Circumcised on the eighth day to put off His flesh and sanctified unto the Lord—Luke 2:21-24; Col. 2:11.
   B. Simeon, a man who was waiting for the consolation of Israel, prophesied to Mary His mother, "Behold, this One is appointed for the falling and rising up of many in Israel and for a sign spoken against— and a sword will pierce through your own soul also—so that the reasonings of many hearts may be revealed"—Luke 2:25, 34-35.
   C. Growing to be strong, filled with wisdom (referring to His deity), and the grace of God (referring to God's grace in His humanity) being upon Him— Luke 2:40.

    D. At the age of twelve He said to His parents, "I must be in the things of My Father," or, "I must be in My Father's house" (Luke 2:49). Early, at the age of twelve, the first God-man was in the things of His Father, that is, in the things concerning His Father's house, which is the church issuing in the Body of Christ, which will consummate the New Jerusalem for the fulfillment of God's eternal economy.

    E. Advancing in wisdom (referring to His deity) and stature (referring to His humanity in stature and age) and in grace manifested in Him before God and men—Luke 2:52.

III. In His silence between the age of twelve and the age of thirty (Luke 3:23):

    A. Growing up like a tender plant before Jehovah and like a root out of dry ground (Isa. 53:2a), indicating that He was of a poor family.

    B. Having no attracting form nor majesty that we should look upon Him, nor beautiful appearance that we should desire Him (Isa. 53:2b), signifying that in both His status and stature He had no dignity of attraction nor desirable appearance.

    C. Being despised and forsaken of men, a man of sorrows and acquainted with grief, respected by no man—Isa. 53:3.

    D. His appearance being marred more than that of any man, and His form more than that of the sons of men—Isa. 52:14.

    E. Tempted in all respects like us, yet without sin—Heb. 4:15b; 2:18.

    All of the states and conditions mentioned above make people silent and inactive in social appearance.

    F. Although the Lord had a concern for God's house when He was at the age of twelve, God did not yet commission Him to carry out the ministry for the purpose to accomplish His eternal economy in taking care of God's house issuing in the Body of Christ, consummating the New Jerusalem.

G. Many servants of God could not tolerate such a time of silence; rather, they failed such a test by God. The real ministry to take care of the house of God issuing in the Body of Christ needs the maturity of age (Num. 4:3).

In this message we want to see the first God-man's living. Many of us know the term *God-man,* but we need to be able to give a clear portion in the New Testament where this God-man is mentioned. We may want to use John 1:14 and Matthew 1:23, but these are not the best verses. John 1:14 says that the Word became flesh. This verse implies the God-man because the Word refers to God Himself who became a man in the flesh. Matthew 1:23 says that the Lord's name would be called Emmanuel, which means God with us. He is God and He is also God incarnated to dwell among us.

But the best verses that reveal the God-man are Romans 1:3 and 4. These verses say that our Lord Jesus Christ was out of the seed of David according to the flesh and was designated the Son of God according to the Spirit of holiness out of the resurrection of the dead. The Son of God is God Himself. Our Christ has two sources and two elements. One is the flesh. The other is the Spirit of holiness. The flesh refers to His humanity. The Spirit of holiness refers to His divinity. This is one Man with two natures—human and divine.

Without Romans 1:3-4, which was spoken by Paul, we would not have a clear view concerning Christ being the first God-man with two natures and two sources. This God-man is the prototype for mass reproduction. He is the first God-man, and we are the many God-men. Second Peter 1:4 says that we are partakers of the divine nature. John 1 tells us that in the Word, which is God, is life, and this life is the light of men shining in the darkness. Whoever would receive this shining receives the life in the Word, and authority is given to him to be a child of God.

If those who are born of God as God's children are not gods, what are they? Are not the children and the Father of the same species? John 3:6 says, "That which is born of the flesh is flesh." Both you and your parents are of the same species, the species of flesh. Verse 6 also says, "That which is born of the Spirit is spirit." The two spirits are of the same species and also of the same source. We are born of God to be the many God-men, the children of God. Also, our

Lord, in whom we believe and whom we worship and follow, is the first God-man.

Genesis 1 speaks of Adam as the first man, and Romans 1 speaks of Christ as the first God-man. Adam's origin was God. The genealogy in Luke 3 says that Adam was the son of God (v. 38). Adam was the son of God because he bore the image of God and God was his origin. In Genesis 1 all things were created according to their kind, their species. But man was created according to God's kind because he was created in God's image and after God's likeness (v. 26). In this sense, Adam was the son of God in image and likeness, but he had only the image of God without the life and nature of God. We are different. We are not only created by God but also born of God, so God is our real, genuine, Father, and we are His real, genuine, children. We have the authority to say that we are the children of God. We have God's image and His life and nature. Romans 8:16 says that the Spirit and our spirit witness together that we are the children of God. This is a great thing. The children of God are the God-men. When we received the Lord Jesus and He came into our spirit, right away an authority was given to us. That authority was the divine life and with this life is the divine nature. We have the life and nature of God because we were born of God to be His children. We are God-men.

We should not forget our status as God-men. This will affect the way that we live. Our admission that we are God-men is not that thorough. If we realize that we are God-men and we mean it, right away we uplift our status. Can a God-man fight with a salesgirl in a department store? In 1968 I was naturalized to be an American citizen, and I began to travel with an American passport. Then I had to behave myself as an American. I had to honor my status. It is the same with our status as God-men. We have sold our status as God-men too cheaply. We need to be brought to a higher level, the level of living the life of a God-man. Most Christians have sold their status as Christians because they live as worldly people. We should be another class of Christians. We are today's God-men because we have been born of God. He is our divine Father, and we are His divine sons. With this realization we could not behave so lightly or speak that freely. Dear saints, whatever our profession is, whether we are teachers or doctors, we should not forget that our status is that of a God-man. A God-man needs to have a God-man living.

The God-man living has a prototype, which should be our example. The first God-man's living was from the manger to the cross. At the beginning and end of His life, there are these two signs. When I was young, I would hesitate to say whether I liked the manger and the cross. But today I feel glorious to say that I am living a life which has the manger at the beginning and the cross at the end. This is the God-man's living. The Lord took the way of humbling Himself, becoming obedient even unto death, the death of the cross (Phil. 2:8). He chose this kind of life, starting with a manger and ending with a cross.

Peter said that since Christ has suffered in His flesh, we also should arm ourselves with the same mind (1 Pet. 4:1). We need to have a strong mind to suffer. Right after I was saved I prayed, "God, from today I want You. I don't want anything else. My whole life will be spent preaching Your gospel. I will bear the Bible and be satisfied with drinking the water from the hills and eating the roots of the trees." That was the start of my Christian life. I was ready to suffer for the Lord's interests, so until today, after about seventy years, nothing of poverty or suffering has ever stumbled me. We must arm ourselves with such a mind, but this should not be out of our natural boldness. This is a following of the Lord Jesus Christ who took this narrow way of a manger and a cross.

I. IN HIS INFANCY

The Lord's infancy shows two things: His lying in a manger (Luke 2:7-16) and His fleeing from His opposers.

A. Lying in a Manger

A baby in a manger, signifying smallness in lowliness, was a sign of the Man-Savior's life (Luke 2:12).

B. Fleeing from His Opposers

He fled from the land of Israel to Egypt (Matt. 2:1-15), and from Egypt back to the land of Israel (vv. 16-21). Then He fled from Bethlehem to Galilee and settled in Nazareth (vv. 22-23). Galilee was a despised province. He became known as the Nazarene. The nickname *Nazarene* came from His fleeing to the insignificant village of Nazareth. I want to help our young people under our training see the pattern of the first God-man's living. We are not training you to be princes to go to big cities. We are training you to flee. My coming to the United States was my fleeing. In the United States I have the freedom of speech to minister all the Lord has shown me for the spreading of the Lord's recovery.

II. IN HIS YOUTH

A. Circumcised on the Eighth Day and Sanctified unto the Lord

In His youth the Lord Jesus was circumcised on the eighth day to put off His flesh and sanctified unto the Lord (Luke 2:21-24; Col. 2:11). Circumcision is a sign that we should not live by our flesh. On the negative side, the Lord was circumcised. On the positive side, He was consecrated to the Lord for His sanctification.

B. The Testimony of Simeon

Also, Simeon, a man who was waiting for Christ as the consolation of Israel, prophesied to Mary His mother, "Behold, this One is appointed [by God] for the falling and rising up of many in Israel and for a sign spoken against—and a sword will pierce through your own soul also—so that the reasonings of many hearts may be revealed" (Luke 2:25, 34-35). From His youth the Lord became a sign spoken against, a kind of center of people's criticizing. If we mean business to consider ourselves God-men, we will be the center of people's talk. What they speak about us will reveal the reasonings in their hearts.

C. Growing to Be Strong

The first God-man grew to be strong; He was filled with wisdom (referring to His deity), and the grace of God (referring to God's grace in His humanity) was upon Him (Luke 2:40). We should expect that our children would grow in this way.

D. Being in the Things
concerning His Father's House

At the age of twelve He said to His parents, "I must be in the things of My Father," or, "I must be in My Father's house" (Luke 2:49). Early, at the age of twelve, the first God-man was in the things of His Father, that is, in the things concerning His Father's house, which is the church issuing in the Body of Christ, which will consummate the New Jerusalem for the fulfillment of God's eternal economy. In God's eternal economy, the center is His house. This house is today's church, this church issues in the Body of Christ, and the Body of Christ consummates the New Jerusalem. When the Lord was only twelve, He had the concern for God's economy. The New Jerusalem is the total end of the entire sixty-six books of the Bible. This holy city is the very organism of the Triune God, constituted with the Triune God and with His redeemed.

God is very thoughtful and purposeful. He has a heart's desire as His good pleasure, so He made an economy. In 1 Timothy 1:3-4 Paul told Timothy to charge certain ones not to teach different things other than the economy of God. In Ephesians 3 we can see what the economy of God is. The economy of God is His plan to distribute the unsearchable riches of Christ to people that the church may be produced (vv. 8-11). This church issues in the Body of Christ, and this Body of Christ is consummated in the New Jerusalem. The New Jerusalem is the consummated Body of Christ and the totality of God's economy. We are here living for this. We have the concern for the Father's house which the Lord Jesus had when He was twelve.

E. Advancing in Wisdom and Stature

The Lord Jesus advanced in wisdom (referring to His deity) and stature (referring to His humanity in stature and age) and in grace manifested in Him before God and men (Luke 2:52). He was growing in this way when He was in His childhood. But today as God-men we all should grow in this way.

III. IN HIS SILENCE BETWEEN THE AGE OF TWELVE AND THE AGE OF THIRTY

A. Growing Up like a Tender Plant before Jehovah and like a Root out of Dry Ground

The Lord's being a root out of dry ground (Isa. 53:2a) meant that He came from a poor family.

B. Having No Dignity of Attraction nor Desirable Appearance

He had no attracting form nor majesty that we should look upon Him, nor beautiful appearance that we should desire Him (Isa. 53:2b), signifying that in both His status and stature He had no dignity of attraction nor desirable appearance.

C. Being Despised and Forsaken of Men

He was despised and forsaken of men, a man of sorrows and acquainted with grief, respected by no man (Isa. 53:3).

D. His Appearance Being Marred More Than That of Any Man

His appearance was marred more than that of any man, and His form more than that of the sons of men (Isa. 52:14).

E. Tempted yet without Sin

He was tempted in all respects like us, yet without sin (Heb. 4:15b; 2:18).

All of the states and conditions mentioned above make people silent and inactive in social appearance. If you are in all these kinds of states and conditions, you have to be silent, because no one honors or appreciates you. To be a very active person in society, to be so social, is dangerous. When the Lord Jesus was on this earth, He did not have this kind of danger. He was despised, undesirable in outward appearance, and not respected by any men.

F. God Not Yet Commissioning Him

Although the Lord had a concern for God's house when He was at the age of twelve, God did not yet commission Him to carry out the ministry for the purpose to accomplish His eternal economy in taking care of God's house issuing in the Body of Christ, consummating the New Jerusalem. Man moves too fast, but God is patient. He told Adam that He would come as the seed of woman to destroy Satan, but He did not come until four thousand years later. When the Lord Jesus was born, that was a fulfillment of God's promise to Adam in Genesis 3:15.

G. The Real Ministry Needing the Maturity of Age

Many servants of God could not tolerate such a time of silence; rather, they failed such a test by God. The real ministry to take care of the house of God issuing in the Body of Christ needs the maturity of life [age] (Num. 4:3). The more maturity you have, the wiser you will be. Elders should be brothers who have grown up to a certain degree in maturity. Then they are qualified to be elders. I hope all of the young people will be trained to go on to grow up according to the pattern of the first God-man, the prototype.

THE GOD-MAN LIVING

MESSAGE FOUR

THE FIRST GOD-MAN'S LIVING
FROM THE MANGER TO THE CROSS

(2)

Scripture Reading: Matt. 3:13-17; 21:32; John 1:14; Rom. 1:3-4; 8:3; Matt. 12:17-19; Heb. 1:9; Matt. 4:1-11

OUTLINE

IV. In His ministry:

    A. The commencement of the first God-man's ministry for the accomplishing of God's eternal economy:

       1. Through His baptism by John the Baptist—Matt. 3:13-17:

         a. To fulfill the righteousness according to the way of righteousness brought in by John—v. 15; 21:32.

         b. Recognizing that, according to His flesh (His humanity—John 1:14; Rom. 1:3; 8:3), He was good for nothing but death and burial.

       2. By God the Father's anointing—vv. 16b-17:

         a. In opening the heavens, indicating that the significance of His baptism was accepted and sealed by the heavens.

         b. In sending His Spirit to descend upon Him, indicating that the Triune God would be one with Him as the source, supply, power, and authority of His ministry.

         c. Declaring to the whole universe, particularly to the angels, that according to the Spirit of holiness (His divinity—Rom. 1:4) He is the Son of God, the Beloved of the Father, in whom is the Father's delight.

       d. Based upon the Father's choosing—Matt. 12:17-19.

       e. Because of His loving of righteousness and hating of lawlessness—Heb. 1:9.

B. His temptations:

  1. At the beginning of His ministry—Matt. 4:1-11:

     a. A temptation under the leading of the Holy Spirit of God arranged by God for the God-man to be tested before His assuming of His ministry—v. 1a.

     b. The temptation of the devil—vv. 1b-10:

        1) The devil, based upon God the Father's saying in His anointing to the God-man that He was God's beloved Son, tempted Him to make a show of Himself being the Son of God for His self-exaltation and self-glorification and to do a miracle to bid the stones to become loaves of bread for His hunger, but the God-man defeated him by not making a show of Himself and not caring for the loaves of bread but for every word of God—vv. 3-4.

        2) Again, the devil, based upon God the Father's saying that the God-man was His beloved Son, tempted the God-man to jump from the wing of the temple so that God would command His angels to bear Him up, but the God-man overcame him by telling him that it is written, "You shall not test the Lord your God"—vv. 5-7.

        3) The devil took the God-man to a very high mountain and showed Him all the kingdoms of the world and their glory and said to Him, "All these will I give You if You will fall down and worship me," but the God-man conquered him by not loving the worldly kingdoms and their glory and saying to the devil, "Go away, Satan! For it is written, 'You shall worship

the Lord your God, and Him only shall you serve'"—vv. 8-10.

c. It was under the leading of the Spirit of God that the first God-man was brought to be tempted by the devil for His test. With the devil, the enemy of God, that temptation was a temptation, but with God, it was a test, and the test became a battle between Satan and God concerning the accomplishment of God's eternal economy. Knowing that God wanted to destroy him by the man, in his flesh, that is, in his humanity, whom he had poisoned and spoiled, Satan took the strategy of tempting the first God-man to assume that He was the Son of God, standing far off from the position of His humanity. Knowing this, the first God-man fought back by saying "man" (v. 4), holding fast the standing of His being a man. This defeated Satan's subtle strategy! Furthermore, in the God-man's second and third fighting back, His answers, "You shall not test the Lord your God" and "You shall worship the Lord your God, and Him only shall you serve" (vv. 7, 10), all were His strongest emphasis that He was a man, a creature of God, dealing with Satan, another creature of God, to take the strongest stand with God for God's glory.

d. The God-man's defeating of the tempter's initial temptation equals His passing of God's test and qualifies Him to be God's Anointed, Messiah, and Christ for God's economy.

e. In this initial warfare Satan's intention was to destroy the One anointed by God for His economy. But he lost the war and left that battleground in shame before the angels of God—v. 11a.

    f. In this initial fighting for God's economy, the first God-man won the war for the glory of God, and the angels of God came triumphantly and ministered to the God-man, taking care of His forty-day fasting hunger—v. 11b.

IV. IN HIS MINISTRY

Matthew 3:13 through 4:11 reveals how the Lord began to live in His ministry, which commenced when He was thirty years old (Luke 3:23). Christ's ministry is not just to save sinners or to do good things but to accomplish God's eternal economy. When He became thirty, God established Him to carry out His ministry for the purpose of accomplishing God's eternal economy.

The end and the ultimate issue of the sixty-six books of the Bible show us the conclusion of God's eternal economy. Genesis ends with Joseph in a coffin, but Exodus ends gloriously with the glorious God in the tabernacle. In the last two chapters of Revelation, which are the end of the entire Scriptures, is a holy city, the New Jerusalem. The Bible, especially the New Testament, has been studied, interpreted, and taught for nearly twenty centuries. We are standing on the shoulders of many who have gone before us and have seen many parts of the divine revelation. Today our interpretation of the Bible is not based upon our narrow view. It is based upon the corporate view of the Body.

When the expositors of the Bible came to the New Jerusalem, it was difficult for them to say whether the New Jerusalem was a literal city or a sign. Revelation 1:1 clearly says that Christ made His revelation known to John by signs. The Lamb, who was Christ, is a sign. The lampstands are signs. For eternity Christ in Revelation is called the Lamb, the Lamb has a wife, and the wife is the city. Revelation 21:9 speaks of the city as the wife of the Lamb. How could a city be a wife? Surely, based upon the principle of the book of Revelation, the holy city is also a sign, signifying the composition of the totality of God's redeemed saints throughout the generations, who have been regenerated, transformed, and glorified. It is not a material, lifeless city but a corporate living person as the bride, having Christ, such a wonderful person, as her Husband. This holy city is the ultimate consummation of God's economy.

A. The Commencement
of the First God-man's Ministry for
the Accomplishing of God's Eternal Economy

As the first God-man, Christ lived on earth in a particular way for the accomplishing of God's eternal economy which ultimately consummates in the New Jerusalem. The very center of the four Gospels is Christ. Matthew 1:18 and 20 say that this God-man's conception was of the Holy Spirit. The God-man was one person, but of two sources. The first source is divine, and the second source is human. He was one person of two natures—human and divine.

The section from the end of Matthew 3 through the beginning of Matthew 4 shows us how this God-man lived and ministered. This one section covers three things: Christ being baptized, Christ being anointed by God, and Christ being tempted by the devil. He was tempted by the devil, but He was led by the Holy Spirit to be tempted by the devil, Satan. Have we ever realized that Christ's temptation was led by the Holy Spirit? In other words, it was the Holy Spirit who put Him into the temptation of the devil. We need to see the intrinsic significance of His being baptized, anointed, and tempted.

Christ started His ministry when He became thirty years of age, the full age God required for anyone to serve Him. All the priests in the Old Testament had to be thirty years of age (Num. 4:3). If you were twenty-five, you could be only an apprentice, a learner, not a full priest. Luke 3 tells us that when Christ became thirty years of age, He came out to minister. Then He was baptized by a man, John the Baptist, anointed by God, and tempted by Satan. Man, God, and Satan were all involved at the beginning of the God-man's ministry.

1. Through His Baptism by John the Baptist

a. To Fulfill the Righteousness
according to the Way of Righteousness Brought In by John

When John the Baptist came, God gave up the Mosaic law. The law was over. John the Baptist came with only one way, the way of righteousness. In Matthew 21:32 the Lord said,

"John came to you in the way of righteousness." We have to pay attention to this expression *the way of righteousness.* Moses came to Israel with many commandments, statutes, and ordinances. Exodus, Leviticus, Numbers, and Deuteronomy cover all of them. But John the Baptist did not bring anything of the law. He came only in the way of righteousness. The way of righteousness is to recognize that you are good for nothing except death and burial.

John's preaching was the beginning of the gospel of Jesus Christ (Mark 1:1). He declared, "Repent, for the kingdom of the heavens has drawn near" (Matt. 3:2). When people repented, he would put them into the water to bury them. John baptized people with water, indicating that man in the flesh is good only for death and burial. But then the Lord Jesus came to put people into the Spirit to have life (v. 11). This is the New Testament.

Christ's ministry commenced by His baptism (vv. 13-17). Before He carried out any part of His ministry, the first thing He did was to be baptized to fulfill the righteousness according to the way of righteousness brought in by John (v. 15; 21:32). This means that even though Israel had all the laws of Moses, they were altogether unrighteous before God. Righteousness became bankrupt among Israel. Moses' law did not help them to be righteous, so God had a new start by sending another man by the name of John. He was different from Moses. Moses was full of culture and education, but John was uncultured and uneducated. He ate wild food and wore wild clothing. Such a one was sent by God to preach the New Testament gospel at the very beginning. He preached by telling people to repent of all their unrighteousness. No one was righteous, so they all had to repent. When they repented, John baptized them, indicating that they were good only for death and burial. After this burial, they were led to One who would come after John. This One would bury them into the Spirit to give them a new life.

b. Recognizing That, according to His Flesh, He Was Good for Nothing but Death and Burial

The Lord Jesus recognized that according to His flesh (His

humanity—John 1:14; Rom. 1:3; 8:3) He was good for nothing but death and burial. Jesus needed to be baptized because He became flesh, and the flesh, in the eyes of God, is good for nothing but death and burial. To bury such a dead person by baptism is the way of righteousness, not the way of the law with its statutes and ordinances.

2. By God the Father's Anointing

Christ's ministry commenced through His baptism and then by God the Father's anointing (Matt. 3:16b-17). The opening of the heavens indicated that the significance of His baptism was accepted and sealed by the heavens. The Father's sending His Spirit to descend upon Him indicated that the Triune God would be one with Him as the source, supply, power, and authority of His ministry. His anointing by God the Father declared to the whole universe, particularly to the angels, that according to the Spirit of holiness (His divinity—Rom. 1:4) He is the Son of God, the Beloved of the Father, in whom is the Father's delight.

In the flesh He was good for nothing but death and burial. But by anointing Him the Father declared something according to another source, the source of the Spirit of holiness, His divinity. The Father declared that this One standing in the water, baptized by John, had two sources: the source of the flesh, His humanity, and the source of the Spirit of holiness, His divinity. According to His humanity He was in the flesh, which was good for nothing but death and burial, but according to His divinity He was the Son of God. In the Old Testament sometimes the angels were called the sons of God. Job 1 speaks of a time when God and the angels had a conference, and it refers to the angels as His sons (v. 6). But Christ is not an angel of God. This One is of the divine source, divinity. God anointed Him and declared, particularly to the angels, that He was the Son of God according to His divinity.

His anointing was based upon the Father's choosing (Matt. 12:17-19) and because of Christ's loving of righteousness and hating of lawlessness (Heb. 1:9). God brought in the way of righteousness, so Christ as a man hated lawlessness and loved righteousness. Because of this God particularly anointed Him.

B. His Temptations

1. At the Beginning of His Ministry

a. Under the Leading of the Holy Spirit of God

At the beginning of His ministry the Lord passed through a temptation under the leading of the Holy Spirit of God arranged by God for the God-man to be tested before His assuming of His ministry (Matt. 4:1-11). Not many have seen that Christ was tempted by the devil under the leading of the Holy Spirit and under the arrangement of God. This anointed One had to be tested by the evil one before He assumed His ministry.

b. The Temptation of the Devil

1) Tempting the God-man to Make a Show of Himself as the Son of God

The devil, based upon God the Father's saying in His anointing to the God-man that He was God's beloved Son, tempted Him to make a show of Himself being the Son of God for His self-exaltation and self-glorification and to do a miracle to bid the stones to become loaves of bread for His hunger, but the God-man defeated him by not making a show of Himself and not caring for the loaves of bread but for every word of God (vv. 3-4). If any of us had been in the Lord's place, we probably would have declared, "I am the Son of God," and then we would have proved it by bidding the stones to become loaves of bread. But Jesus Christ did not take the devil's temptation. He was the Son of God, but He did not need to make a show of it. He took the position of a man, who lives not only by bread but also by every word of God. He cared only for God's interests, not for His need. This is the intrinsic significance of the first part of the devil's temptation.

2) Tempting the God-man to Jump from the Wing of the Temple

Again, the devil, based upon God the Father's saying that the God-man was His beloved Son, tempted the God-man to jump from the wing of the temple so that God would command His angels to bear Him up, but the God-man overcame him by

telling him that it is written, "You shall not test the Lord your
God" (vv. 5-7). The devil tempted the Lord again to perform a
miracle that would exalt and glorify the self, but the God-man
overcame him by telling him that He as a man should not test
the Lord His God. He was standing on His position as a man,
and He did not want to do anything to show that He was the
Son of God.

Those who are young in the Lord's recovery or in the
ministry always want to do something marvelous. You may
go to a new place and desire to have gospel meetings with
many people getting saved and with miracles. But we need
to realize that this is a temptation to exalt and glorify the
self. Any thought of doing miraculous things in religion for
self-exaltation is a temptation of the devil. The Lord Jesus
said, "Many will say to Me in that day, Lord, Lord, was it
not in Your name that we prophesied, and in Your name cast
out demons, and in Your name did many works of power?
And then I will declare to them: I never knew you. Depart
from Me, you workers of lawlessness" (7:22-23).

3) Tempting the God-man
with the Kingdoms of the World and Their Glory

The devil took the God-man to a very high mountain and
showed Him all the kingdoms of the world and their glory
and said to Him, "All these will I give You if You will fall
down and worship me," but the God-man conquered him by
not loving the worldly kingdoms and their glory and saying
to the devil, "Go away, Satan! For it is written, 'You shall
worship the Lord your God, and Him only shall you serve'"
(4:8-10). The Lord defeated the devil by standing on the
ground of man to worship and serve only God.

c. Brought to Be Tempted by the Devil
under the Leading of the Spirit

It was under the leading of the Spirit of God that the first
God-man was brought to be tempted by the devil for His test.
With the devil, the enemy of God, that temptation was a
temptation, but with God, it was a test, and the test became a
battle between Satan and God concerning the accomplishment

of God's eternal economy. Knowing that God wanted to destroy him by the man, in his flesh, that is, in his humanity, whom he had poisoned and spoiled, Satan took the strategy of tempting the first God-man to assume that He was the Son of God, standing far off from the position of His humanity. Knowing this, the first God-man fought back by saying "man" (v. 4), holding fast the standing of His being a man. This defeated Satan's subtle strategy! Furthermore, in the God-man's second and third fighting back, His answers, "You shall not test the Lord your God" and "You shall worship the Lord your God, and Him only shall you serve" (vv. 7, 10), all were His strongest emphasis that He was a man, a creature of God, dealing with Satan, another creature of God, to take the strongest stand with God for God's glory. God would not deal with Satan as his Creator. Instead, God dealt with him by another creature, man. Satan tried his best to tempt this man to stay away from His position as a man. But the Lord Jesus stood in man's position firmly to glorify God and accomplish God's economy.

d. Qualifying Him to Be
God's Anointed, Messiah, and Christ

The God-man's defeating of the tempter's initial temptation equals His passing of God's test and qualifies Him to be God's Anointed, Messiah, among Israel, and Christ among Christians for God's economy.

e. Satan's Losing the War

In this initial warfare Satan's intention was to destroy the One anointed by God for His economy. But he lost the war and left that battleground in shame before the angels of God (v. 11a).

f. The First God-man
Winning the War for the Glory of God

In this initial fighting for God's economy, the first God-man won the war for the glory of God, and the angels of God came triumphantly and ministered to the God-man, taking care of His forty-day fasting hunger (v. 11b).

THE GOD-MAN LIVING

MESSAGE FIVE

A WORD OF DEFINITION

(1)

OUTLINE

I. The way of righteousness:
   Scripture Reading:
   Matt. 21:32: "John came to you in the way of righteousness."

   A. The Old Testament dispensation of law ended at the commencement of the first God-man's ministry:
      1. The law of the Old Testament dispensation charged man to do good according to the law that man might be justified by God according to His law (Lev. 18:5), yet men sought to establish their own righteousness, not subject to the righteousness of God—Rom. 10:3, 5.
      2. The outcome of the law was that man was exposed to be sinful before the righteous God (Rom. 4:15; 5:20; Gal. 3:19) and no man of the flesh could be justified by God (Rom. 3:20).

   B. The New Testament dispensation, the dispensation of grace, that is, the dispensation of the gospel of Jesus Christ, began from the preaching of John the Baptist—Mark 1:1-4:
      1. John came in the way of righteousness and preached, "Repent, for the kingdom of the heavens has drawn near"—Matt. 3:2.
      2. John charged the people to repent because of the kingdom of the heavens. The kingdom of God is of righteousness (Rom. 14:17), and the kingdom of the heavens is particularly based

upon righteousness (Matt. 5:20). This righteousness is the foundation of God's throne (Psa. 89:14).

3. When the people received John's preaching and came to repent to him, he right away baptized them by putting them into the water to bury them, indicating that they were men of the flesh who had nothing good (Rom. 7:18) and were worthy only of death and burial.

4. Following John's ministry, Jesus Christ came and baptized these people with the Spirit, joining them, in resurrection, to God, who saved them by justifying them according to His righteousness—Rom. 1:17; 3:21-25; 1 Cor. 1:30.

5. Furthermore, after He died judicially for these repentant people, Christ resurrected to live within them that they may live by Christ's life a life of righteousness to be justified by God all the time—Rom. 4:25.

6. All these people are called "the righteous" who will shine forth like the sun in the coming kingdom (Matt. 13:43), and their righteousness will abide in the new heavens and new earth forever (2 Pet. 3:13).

7. Thus, to repent and be baptized according to John's preaching and practice was ordained by God according to the righteous requirements of God's eternal economy; hence, it is to fulfill the righteousness of God (Matt. 3:15) as a matter of eternity.

II. The proper and righteous base of Jesus' baptism:
Scripture Reading:
Matt. 3:13-15: "Then Jesus came from Galilee to the Jordan to John to be baptized by him. But John tried to prevent Him, saying, It is I who have need of being baptized by You, and You come to me? But Jesus answered and said to him, Permit it for now, for it is fitting for us in this way to fulfill all righteousness. Then he permitted Him."

A. The base for Jesus to be baptized is that He considered Himself, according to His humanity, a man, especially an Israelite, who is a man "in the flesh" (John 1:14). Even though He was only "in the likeness of the flesh of sin" (Rom. 8:3), "without sin" (Heb. 4:15), yet He was "in the flesh," which has nothing good but is worthy only of death and burial.

B. Based upon this fact, at the beginning of His ministry for God, He was willing to be baptized by John the Baptist, recognizing that, according to His humanity, He was one who did not have any qualification to be a servant of God.

C. As a man in the flesh, He needed to be a dead man buried in the death water to fulfill God's New Testament requirement according to His righteousness, and He did it willingly, considering it the fulfilling of God's righteousness. Such a base surely is proper and righteous.

In this message we want to give a word of definition concerning the way of righteousness and concerning the proper and righteous base of Jesus' baptism. When I was young, I wondered why the Lord Jesus, who was not a sinner, needed to be baptized. This question has been remaining within me for about seventy years. It was not until writing the outlines for these messages that I found the answer.

Also, I would like to point out that to study the first God-man's living is actually to study all the temptations through which He passed. The four Gospels are a record of His temptations. He was tempted, tested, by the devil Satan, the Pharisees, Sadducees, and Herodians. Even the Lord's fleshly brothers tested Him. Wherever He went and with whomever He contacted, there were temptations. To be a Christian, in a sense, is not an easy thing. This is because God and we have an opposing party, Satan.

It is not easy to understand why God lets Satan be so free. According to Isaiah 14, God has judged Satan (vv. 12-15). Also, according to Hebrews 2:14, Christ destroyed him on the cross. God condemned him with a strong verdict, and Christ destroyed him, but why is he still so free today? I would answer this by asking another question—without Satan, how could God test us? Satan even tested God, and God even invited Satan to test Him. He said to Satan, "Have you considered My servant Job?" (Job 1:8, NASB). After Satan challenged the Lord, He gave Satan the permission to test Job, saying, "All that he has is in your power, only do not put forth your hand on him" (v. 12). Job then passed through a time of testing which nearly no one could stand. In God's economy, He arranged to have an enemy, a testing one, who had been a cherub created by God, appointed by God, and even anointed by God.

I. THE WAY OF RIGHTEOUSNESS

Matthew 21:32 says, "John came to you in the way of righteousness." In the Old Testament, Moses came in the way of condemnation. Second Corinthians 3 says clearly that the Old Testament ministry was a ministry of condemnation and that the New Testament ministry is a ministry of righteousness

(v. 9). The entire New Testament is a matter of righteousness. John the Baptist does not belong to the Old Testament. Some have said that John was a transitional person who was neither in the Old Testament nor in the New Testament, but this is wrong. Mark 1 reveals that the gospel of Jesus Christ began from John the Baptist. John's teaching was the commencement of God's New Testament economy.

A. The Old Testament Dispensation of Law Ending at the Commencement of the First God-man's Ministry

1. Charging Man to Do Good according to the Law

The law of the Old Testament dispensation charged man to do good according to the law that man might be justified by God according to His law (Lev. 18:5), yet men sought to establish their own righteousness, not subject to the righteousness of God (Rom. 10:3, 5).

2. The Outcome of the Law

The outcome of the law was that man was exposed to be sinful before the righteous God (Rom. 4:15; 5:20; Gal. 3:19) and no man of the flesh could be justified by God (Rom. 3:20). The law did not help God's people become righteous. Instead, it exposed them. No one could do good things to be justified by God. On the contrary, all were exposed. No man of the flesh could be justified by God. The result, the outcome, of the law was absolutely different from what the law expected.

B. The New Testament Dispensation

The New Testament dispensation is the dispensation of grace, unlike the dispensation of the Old Testament, which was the dispensation of the law. The entire New Testament is the dispensation of grace, which is the dispensation of the gospel of Jesus Christ. This dispensation began from the preaching of John the Baptist. This is proved by Mark 1:1-4: "The beginning of the gospel of Jesus Christ, the Son of God, even as it is written in Isaiah the prophet: 'Behold, I send

My messenger before Your face, who will prepare Your way, a voice of one crying in the wilderness: Prepare the way of the Lord; make straight His paths.' John came baptizing in the wilderness and preaching a baptism of repentance for forgiveness of sins." John's coming out to preach his gospel was counted as the beginning of the gospel of Jesus Christ.

1. John Coming in the Way of Righteousness

John came in the way of righteousness and preached, "Repent, for the kingdom of the heavens has drawn near" (Matt. 3:2). The Israelites who were under the ministry of the law of Moses needed to repent because they were all practicing unrighteousness. The record of the society of Israel in Isaiah 1 shows how evil the people had become. The evils seen in Gentile society could also be seen in Israel's society.

2. The Kingdom of God Being of Righteousness

There was no righteousness among the Israelites, so they needed to repent. John charged the people to repent because of the kingdom of the heavens. The kingdom of God is of righteousness (Rom. 14:17), and the kingdom of the heavens is particularly based upon righteousness. In Matthew 5:20 the Lord said, "Unless your righteousness surpasses that of the scribes and Pharisees, you shall by no means enter into the kingdom of the heavens." This righteousness is the foundation of God's throne (Psa. 89:14).

3. Men of Flesh
Being Worthy Only of Death and Burial

When the people received John's preaching and came to repent to him, he right away baptized them by putting them into the water to bury them, indicating that they were men of the flesh who had nothing good (Rom. 7:18) and were worthy only of death and burial. Perhaps some people thought that there should be a good result after their repenting to John. Instead, John put them into the water to bury them, indicating that they were good for nothing. I believe this was why the Pharisees and Sadducees would not come to John. The Gospels show us that there were disciples of three parties: those of John the Baptist, those of the Pharisees, and those of the Sadducees. Those of John the Baptist were a real test to the Pharisees and the Sadducees, so none of them dared to come to John.

The first thought of the New Testament dispensation of grace, the dispensation of the gospel of Jesus Christ, is that all fallen men of the flesh are worthy of nothing except death and burial. This is very serious. Regretfully, many in today's Christianity give people a wrong concept in their preaching of the gospel. We must have people preaching the gospel today who are like John the Baptist, calling people to repent.

4. Jesus Christ Baptizing People with the Spirit

Following John's ministry, Jesus Christ came and baptized these people with the Spirit, joining them, in resurrection, to God, who saved them by justifying them according to His righteousness (Rom. 1:17; 3:21-25; 1 Cor. 1:30). The New Testament begins with the thought of John's preaching, that is, that men of the flesh are good only for death and burial. But this is not the thought of the entire New Testament gospel. This is just the beginning. This thought is continued with the Lord Jesus' coming to practice another kind of baptism. He baptized people into the Spirit to join them in resurrection to God. In baptism there is the practice of burial into water and then a rising up from the water, signifying resurrection. Through death and burial we are finished, but then there is a resurrection. In resurrection, Jesus joins us to God. This thought is greater than death and burial.

The first thought of the New Testament gospel is that every fallen man of the flesh is good for nothing except death and burial, and the second thought is that if you recognize this, Jesus Christ will come to baptize you into the living God, joining you to God in resurrection. This saves you by justifying you according to His righteousness. The Baptizer, Christ, joins you to God to make you one with God, who is righteousness. God would justify you only by His righteousness.

Romans 1:16 and 17 say that the gospel is the power of God that saves both Israel and the Gentiles because the righteousness of God is revealed in it. Baptism is so powerful because Jesus joins the baptized ones to God to make them God in life and nature but not in the Godhead. When a poor wife is joined to her millionaire husband in marriage, they become one. She may have been a poor girl, but at the moment they are joined in marriage she becomes a millionaire. This is what happened when we were joined to God in baptism.

John the Baptist's ministry is to deal with our real situation, which is that we are men of the flesh who are worthy only of death and burial. But Christ, another baptizer, came and joined us to God in resurrection. We were resurrected with Christ to be one with God. Now we are "millionaires" who are joined to another person. This is the second thought of the New Testament gospel of grace. The righteous God gave Himself to us as our righteousness, and this righteousness justified us.

5. Living within Them
That They May Live a Life of Righteousness

Furthermore, after He died judicially for these repentant people, Christ resurrected to live within them that they may live by Christ's life a life of righteousness to be justified by God all the time. This is why Romans 4:25 says that He was raised for our justification. We do not have a dead Savior. We have a Savior who is living, and as the living Spirit, He lives in us. By His life, we have a living that God has to justify all the time. This is the God-man living.

God, the righteous One, gave Himself to us as our righteousness. In the same principle, Christ is given to us as our righteousness. Christ and God are one. First Corinthians 1:30 says Christ, who is given to us, is our righteousness. Christ also has His own righteous act. Romans 5:18 says that Christ's one righteous act was unto justification of life to all men. By His one righteous act of dying on the cross, we all have been justified. Christ has His own righteousness, which qualifies Him to be our Savior.

Some make the mistake of confusing Christ's personal righteous act with Christ Himself, the person. When we compiled our hymnal (Hymns), we corrected all such mistakes in the hymns. Hymn #295 by Zinzendorf said, "Jesus, Thy

blood and righteousness / My beauty are, my glorious dress."
We corrected this to read: "God's Christ, who is my righteousness, / My beauty is, my glorious dress." Christ, the
person, is our righteousness.

6. *"The Righteous" Shining Forth like the Sun*
in the Coming Kingdom

All these people are called "the righteous" who will shine
forth like the sun in the coming kingdom (Matt. 13:43), and
their righteousness will abide in the new heavens and new
earth forever (2 Pet. 3:13). The righteous are also referred to
in Matthew 10:41 and Luke 14:14, and the way of righteousness is spoken of in 2 Peter 2:21. Luke 14:14 speaks of the
resurrection of the righteous. Second Peter 2:21 speaks of
the rebellious ones who knew the way of righteousness but
turned away from God. The New Testament dispensation of
grace is to produce the God-man living, and the God-man
living is a life of righteousness.

7. *Fulfilling the Righteousness of God*
by Repenting and Being Baptized

Thus, to repent and be baptized according to John's
preaching and practice was ordained by God according to the
righteous requirements of God's eternal economy; hence, it
is to fulfill the righteousness of God (Matt. 3:15) as a matter
of eternity. To be baptized is to keep God's New Testament
ordinance, to recognize yourself before God according to His
evaluation and to fulfill God's righteous requirement.

II. THE PROPER AND RIGHTEOUS BASE
OF JESUS' BAPTISM

Matthew 3:13-15 reveals the proper and righteous base of
Jesus' baptism: "Then Jesus came from Galilee to the Jordan
to John to be baptized by him. But John tried to prevent
Him, saying, It is I who have need of being baptized by You,
and You come to me? But Jesus answered and said to him,
Permit it for now, for it is fitting for us in this way to fulfill
all righteousness. Then he permitted Him."

A. The Base for Jesus to Be Baptized

The base for Jesus to be baptized is that He considered Himself, according to His humanity, a man, especially an Israelite, who is a man "in the flesh" (John 1:14). Even though He was only "in the likeness of the flesh of sin" (Rom. 8:3), "without sin" (Heb. 4:15), yet He was "in the flesh," which has nothing good but is worthy only of death and burial. Christ as the Word of God became flesh and *flesh* is a negative term. Of course, Romans 8:3 tells us that He was only in the likeness of the flesh of sin, but He was still in the flesh. This was His standing in His humanity. John the Baptist came out to preach repentance to people in the flesh. Jesus admitted He was in the flesh. Whatever He had according to the flesh was only good for death and burial. He was standing on that ground, and that ground became His base for Him to be baptized.

B. Willing to Be Baptized by John the Baptist

Based upon this fact, at the beginning of His ministry for God, Jesus was willing to be baptized by John the Baptist, recognizing that, according to His humanity, He was one who did not have any qualification to be a servant of God. Jesus stood according to His real situation. His real situation was that He was a man of flesh.

C. Needing to Be a Dead Man

As a man in the flesh, He needed to be a dead man buried in the death water to fulfill God's New Testament requirement according to His righteousness, and He did it willingly, considering it the fulfilling of God's righteousness. Such a base surely is proper and righteous.

THE GOD-MAN LIVING

A WORD OF DEFINITION

(2)

OUTLINE

III. The devil's first stratagem in tempting the first God-man to ignore His human status of being a man—Matt. 4:3-4:

A. In His anointing the first God-man, God declared that He was His beloved Son—Matt. 3:17.

B. Based upon God's declaration that the first God-man was His beloved Son, the devil exercised his first stratagem, tempting the first God-man to ignore that He was a man.

C. But the first God-man defeated His tempter by standing firmly in His position of a man and answering him by saying, "Man shall not live...," insisting to indicate that He was a man—Matt. 4:4.

IV. The devil's second stratagem in tempting the first God-man to assume His divinity of being the Son of God—Matt. 4:5-7:

A. Again, it was based upon what God declared the first God-man was.

B. The devil exercised his second stratagem, tempting the first God-man to assume His divinity by having a miracle of protection by the angels.

C. But the first God-man overcame His subtle tempter by saying, "You shall not test the Lord your God," indicating strongly that He was a man before God who should not test the Lord His God.

D. God in His eternal economy wanted to have a man as one of His creatures to deal with His enemy

Satan, another creature, but the enemy tempted the first God-man to assume His divinity as the Creator of all things. By this subtle way, Satan mixed up the levels of God as the Creator and Satan himself as a creature.

V. The devil's third stratagem in seducing the first God-man to love the glory of the kingdoms of the world, worshipping him as God and serving him as his subordinate—Matt. 4:8-11; Luke 4:5-8:

A. It should have been that in the preadamic age, God appointed the archangel to be the head of the preadamic age (Ezek. 28:13-14), and the authority and glory of the kingdoms of the earth should have been given to him. After he rebelled against God and became God's enemy, Satan, he was judged by God (Isa. 14:12-15), but the full execution of God's judgment upon him will not be completed until the end of the millennium (Rev. 20:7-10). Hence, until that time he has authority over the kingdoms of the earth.

B. In his subtle temptation of the Lord, he offered the earthly kingdoms and their glory to the first God-man as a bait to hook Him so that He would worship him as God and serve him as his subordinate.

C. But the first God-man saw through the evil tempter's devilish device and conquered him by chasing him away and telling him in a shaming way that as a man before God He would worship God and serve Him only.

In the previous message, we saw the definitions of the way of righteousness and the proper and righteous base of Jesus' baptism. Jesus received the baptism by John the Baptist, standing on the base of realizing that He was a man in the flesh. Of course, Jesus had no sin. Romans 8:3 says that He was in the likeness of the flesh of sin, but He was still in the flesh, which in the eyes of God is altogether condemned, rejected, and worthy only of death and burial. Jesus stood on this base to receive the baptism from John.

Before the Lord Jesus began to do anything for His ministry, the first thing He did was to come to John to receive such a baptism to declare to the whole universe that He did not depend at all upon the flesh for God's ministry. We all have to see this. No one should bring anything of his natural life, anything of his flesh, into God's ministry. Especially the co-workers and elders need to realize that as a natural man in the flesh, we are good for nothing except death and burial. We need to have ourselves absolutely terminated in the water of baptism. This is the intrinsic significance of the base of Jesus' baptism. I hope also that all the full-time trainees, spiritually speaking, have accepted such a baptism. We all should declare in our life and work: "I am a person in the flesh, worthy of nothing in the eyes of God but death and burial; so I want to have myself terminated, crucified and buried."

In this message we want to go on to see three definitions covering the three sections of the enemy's one temptation of the first God-man.

III. THE DEVIL'S FIRST STRATAGEM IN TEMPTING THE FIRST GOD-MAN TO IGNORE HIS HUMAN STATUS OF BEING A MAN

Jesus was led to fast for forty days. After the forty days, He was hungry. Then the tempter, Satan, said to Him, "If You are the Son of God, speak that these stones may become loaves of bread" (Matt. 4:3). It was as if Satan were saying to Jesus, "God appointed You and declared that You were His beloved Son, the Son of God, when You were standing in the waters of baptism. If You are such a Son of God, give the word for these stones to become loaves of bread."

I believe we would have failed such a test. We would have performed a miracle to display to everyone that we are the sons of God. But if the Lord had done this, it would have been against the base of His baptism. He came to the wilderness to be tempted as a man, not as the Son of God. The Son of God is just God Himself. Who can tempt God? Jesus was a man in the wilderness. As God Himself, could He be hungry? With God there is no hunger, but as a man Jesus was hungry. Satan's stratagem was to tempt Jesus to ignore His standing as a man and to assume His position as the Son of God. So the Lord answered him by saying, "It is written, 'Man shall not live on bread alone, but on every word that proceeds out through the mouth of God'" (v. 4). He defeated the enemy by His standing as a man.

In His anointing the first God-man, God declared that He was His beloved Son (Matt. 3:17). Based upon God's declaration that the first God-man was His beloved Son, the devil exercised his first stratagem, tempting the first God-man to ignore that He was a man. But the first God-man defeated His tempter by standing firmly in His position of a man and answering him by saying, "Man shall not live...," insisting to indicate that He was a man.

Now we need to consider the application of the devil's first stratagem to our own situation. When some co-workers visit another place, they may expect that the elders there will welcome them as the top co-workers in the recovery and ask them to give a message. What would we do in such a situation? Would we accept this invitation or stand on the base that we are men in the flesh? We should have the attitude that we have nothing good and are worthy only of death and burial. Suppose we take the chance to speak and speak successfully. Then we could declare, "I am a real son of God." Is this what we should stand on? We should stand on the base that we are men in the flesh. What we have is not worth anything in the eyes of God except death and burial.

After passing through two years of training, the full-time trainees may feel that they are special when they return to their localities. Perhaps they expect that everyone will come out in a parade to welcome them back. Even the elders may feel this way because they are so natural. They would announce to the congregation that a certain trainee has returned, and they would ask him to give a message. The returning trainee may feel that this is his golden opportunity to show that he is a son of God. In principle this is the same as Satan's temptation of the Lord to make the stones loaves of bread.

On the other hand, if a trainee returns to his locality and nobody pays any attention to him, he may be disappointed and not know what to do or where to go. Where should you go? Go to the water to die and be buried there. Such a temptation is a test. The Greek word is the same for both *temptation* and *test*. With God it is a test; with the enemy it is a temptation. When we pass through the temptation of the enemy, we pass through the test of God to be approved by God. The first stratagem of the enemy is to annul our proper standing and encourage us to assume a higher standing. Some sisters may become jealous of others who receive more amens than they do in response to their prayer. This means that they need another burial. We all need to realize that in our flesh we are worthy of nothing except death and burial.

IV. THE DEVIL'S SECOND STRATAGEM
IN TEMPTING THE FIRST GOD-MAN TO ASSUME HIS DIVINITY OF BEING THE SON OF GOD

After the devil's first stratagem, his temptation of the first God-man changed somewhat (Matt. 4:5-7). He brought Jesus to the wing of the temple, a very high place. The tempter said to Jesus, "If You are the Son of God, cast Yourself down; for it is written, 'To His angels He shall give charge concerning You, and on their hands they shall bear You up, lest You strike Your foot against a stone'" (v. 6). This was a temptation enticing Jesus to show that as the Son of God He was able to act miraculously. Many of the so-called healings in Pentecostalism are just for the purpose of making a show and are not genuine. We may be attracted by the Lord and react to His attraction by loving and following Him, but at the same time we may desire to have a name like the Son of God and a position like the divine position of God. This is our trouble.

The devil's second stratagem was again based upon what God declared that the first God-man was. The devil then exercised his second stratagem. The first one was to tempt the Lord to ignore His position as a man and to assume His divine position as the Son of God by performing a miracle. When this did not work, the devil tried to make Him assume His position in divinity to display His power and His authority by having a miracle of protection by the angels. But the first God-man overcame His subtle tempter by saying, "You shall not test the Lord your God" (v. 7), indicating strongly that He was a man before God who should not test the Lord His God. Not to test means not to tempt. He, the first God-man, stood on the ground of a creature, recognizing that God was His Lord. He declared, "I shall not tempt My Lord. He is My Lord." In being tempted the Lord had at least three statuses: first He was a man, second a creature, and third the Son of God. As a man, He could not test His Lord.

God in His eternal economy wanted to have a man as one of His creatures to deal with His enemy Satan, another creature, but the enemy tempted the first God-man to assume His divinity as the Creator of all things. By this subtle way, Satan mixed up the levels of God as the Creator and Satan himself as a creature. We can see this when Jesus indicated that as a man, God's creature, He would not test the Lord, His Creator. Today we must realize first that we are a man of the flesh worthy of nothing and second that we are a creature. God desires to use a creature to deal with Satan, another creature. Here we can see God's wisdom. God would never deal with Satan directly. According to Hebrews 2:14, the Lord Jesus destroyed Satan by partaking of the flesh. He destroyed Satan in His flesh. Christ, as a creature, not as the Creator, destroyed Satan. He destroyed Satan as a creature on the same level as Satan. By this, He honored God's unique position as the Creator. Satan's way was to uplift himself to the level of the Creator.

V. THE DEVIL'S THIRD STRATAGEM IN SEDUCING THE FIRST GOD-MAN TO LOVE THE GLORY OF THE KINGDOMS OF THE WORLD, WORSHIPPING HIM AS GOD AND SERVING HIM AS HIS SUBORDINATE

After his first two stratagems failed, Satan tried a third time to tempt the Lord to love the glory of the kingdoms of the world, worshipping him as God and serving him as his subordinate (Matt. 4:8-11; Luke 4:5-8).

The enemy would tempt us to love the world by getting us to consider how successful the people in the world are, while we are nothing. I began to serve the Lord with my full time in 1933. About ten years later, I was imprisoned by the invading Japanese army and afterward I contracted tuberculosis of the lungs. One day while I was still recuperating from my illness, I was walking with a stick on a bridge and a thought came to me saying, "You've been laboring for your Lord for ten years. What have you gained? All you have is a stick in your hand and nothing else. But look at how successful your classmates and other people have become." That was a temptation. Many cannot overcome the third stratagem of the enemy: to use the world as a bait to hook us. I have seen many get hooked by this bait.

It should have been that in the preadamic age God appointed the archangel to be the head of the preadamic age (Ezek. 28:13-14), and the authority and glory of the kingdoms of the earth should have been given to him. After he rebelled against God and became God's enemy, Satan, he was judged by God (Isa. 14:12-15), but the full execution of God's judgment upon him will not be completed until the end of the millennium (Rev. 20:7-10). Hence, until that time he has authority over the kingdoms of the earth. In his subtle temptation of the Lord, he offered the earthly kingdoms and their glory to the first God-man as a bait to hook Him so that He would worship him as God and serve him as his subordinate. But the first God-man saw through the evil tempter's devilish device and conquered him by chasing him away and telling him in a shaming way that as a man before God He would worship God and serve Him only.

I hope that these definitions will help us to see Satan's stratagems. All of us are under these dangers. Every day our enemy is busy, and he is very diligent.

THE GOD-MAN LIVING

MESSAGE SEVEN

THE FIRST GOD-MAN'S LIVING
FROM THE MANGER TO THE CROSS

(3)

Scripture Reading: Matt. 22:15-46; 26:57-68

OUTLINE

IV. In His ministry:

  B. His temptations:

    2. During His ministry—Matt. 22:15-46:

      a. The tempter's intention—to ensnare Him in His words—v. 15.

      b. By the Pharisees with the Herodians—vv. 16-22:

        1) The Pharisees were the fundamentalists of Judaism.

        2) The Herodians were the political party under King Herod for Roman imperialism, usurped by the Pharisees in tempting the first God-man.

        3) They tempted Him by asking whether it was lawful to give tribute to Caesar, the emperor of Rome, trying to catch Him as one who was against imperialistic Rome—v. 17.

        4) He asked them to show Him the coin for the tribute. When they showed Him, He asked them whose image and inscription were on the coin; they answered, "Caesar's." He answered them, "Render then the things that are Caesar's to Caesar

and the things that are God's to God."
He defeated them in their plot—vv. 18-22.

c. By the Sadducees—vv. 23-34:

   1) The Sadducees were the modernists at their time in the Jewish religion, not believing in the resurrection.

   2) They tempted the first God-man by telling Him that among them there were seven brothers who married one woman consecutively. Then they asked Him whose wife this woman would be in the resurrection. He said that they erred and did not know the Scriptures nor the power of God, for in the resurrection they neither marry nor are given in marriage, but are like angels in heaven. He taught them that God as the God of Abraham, the God of Isaac, and the God of Jacob is not the God of the dead, but of the living. By this He muzzled their mouths—vv. 23-34.

d. By a lawyer of the Pharisees—vv. 34-40:

   1) A lawyer of the Pharisees, knowing that the first God-man muzzled the mouths of the Sadducees, tested Him by asking Him which is the great commandment in the law—vv. 34-36.

   2) He answered, "'You shall love the Lord your God with all your heart and with all your soul and with all your mind.' This is the great and first commandment. And the second is like it: 'You shall love your neighbor as yourself.' On these two commandments hang all the Law and the Prophets." By this He conquered them also—vv. 37-40.

e. The first God-man turned the test to them—vv. 41-46:

   1) He tested them by saying, "What do you think concerning the Christ? Whose son

is He?" They answered, "David's." He said, "How then does David in spirit call Him Lord [Psa. 110:1]...? If then David calls Him Lord, how is He his son?"—vv. 41-45.

2) Not one of them was able to answer Him a word, nor did anyone from that day dare to question Him anymore—v. 46.

3) The Pharisees, the Herodians, the Sadducees, and a lawyer of the Pharisees tempted the first God-man with questions concerning Roman imperialism, the belief of the Jewish religion, and their creed, thinking that they could ensnare Him, but He defeated them all by His wise and subduing answers, which led them to consider the person of Christ who, not the political and religious things, was their real need.

4) When He tested them with the person of Christ, they did not have the adequate knowledge, knowing Christ only in His humanity as the seed of David but not in His divinity as the Lord of David, who will sit at the right hand of God (Psa. 110:1). Eventually, He muzzled all their mouths and won the victory in the mutual testings.

3. At the end of His ministry—Matt. 26:57-68:

a. In the time of His being judged by the Jewish Sanhedrin after He was arrested by the Roman authorities in the night—vv. 57-58.

b. They tested Him about several things so that they might put Him to death, but He answered nothing—vv. 59-62.

c. Eventually, the high priest tested Him concerning whether He was the Christ, the Son of God—v. 63.

d. He answered, "You have said rightly. Nevertheless I say to you, From now on you will see the Son of Man sitting at the right hand of Power [Psa. 110:1] and coming on the clouds of heaven"—v. 64.

e. The high priest tore his garments and said that He had blasphemed, and the Sanhedrin considered that He was worthy of death—vv. 65-66.

f. They spit in His face and beat Him with their fists, and others slapped Him—vv. 67-68.

g. In the last temptation of the first God-man by the high priest usurped by Satan, the high priest's test was in principle the same as the devil's in the beginning of the temptations, tempting the first God-man to assume His divine position as the Son of God and ignore His human position as a man—Matt. 4:3-7.

h. The first God-man, knowing the stratagem of Satan, in His answer again did not assume His divine position as the Son of God but strongly stressed His human position as the Son of Man to shame Satan and annul him by His humanity.

4. In conclusion, all the temptations by Satan and his usurped instruments present us a vivid picture that the first God-man behaved stately within the limit of His positions according to His dual status of God and man. His wisdom, His honesty, His faithfulness to God, His sobermindedness concerning His position and status, and His conquering and subduing ability, all were shown in this ugly portrait of His enemy Satan, the devil. The actual result of the temptations by the opposers of the first God-man did afford a chance for Him to unveil to them the person of Christ in full, that He is both God as the Lord of David, their

respected father, and man, a seed of David, who will sit at the right hand of God (Psa. 110:1). Such an all-inclusive Christ was the real need for their life, but what a pity that they were blinded by Satan and became ignorant of their real need so that they despised Him, forsook Him, and sentenced Him to death by crucifixion! (Matt. 26:66-67).

In the previous message we saw the devil's stratagems in tempting the Lord at the beginning of His ministry. In this message we want to see the temptations suffered by the Lord during His ministry and at the end of His ministry. Although the Lord passed through some other temptations, the principles are all covered by these three categories of temptations. I hope that we would pay our full attention to the fellowship in this message and even study it with some others.

B. His Temptations

2. *During His Ministry*

Matthew 22:15-46 shows the temptations through which the Lord passed during His ministry.

a. The Tempter's Intention

The tempter's intention was to ensnare Him in His words (v. 15).

b. By the Pharisees with the Herodians

The Pharisees were the fundamentalists of Judaism. The Herodians were the political party under King Herod for Roman imperialism, usurped by the Pharisees in tempting the first God-man. They tempted Him by asking whether it was lawful to give tribute to Caesar, the emperor of Rome, trying to catch Him as one who was against imperialistic Rome (vv. 16-17). The Pharisees were for the Jews, whereas the Herodians were for the Romans. Such a question concerning whether or not to give tribute to Caesar was hard to answer. If the Lord said yes, he would offend the Jews. If He said no, that would offend Rome. That was really an ensnaring question. But the Lord's capacity was so high, His wisdom was so deep, and His answer was very subduing.

He asked them to show Him the coin for the tribute. This means that He did not have any coin from Caesar and asked them to give Him one. Their having a Roman coin in their pocket meant that they had lost the case already. The Lord Jesus did not show the Roman coin but asked them to show one to Him. Since they possessed one of the Roman coins, they were caught. When they showed Him, He asked them whose image and inscription were on the coin; they answered, "Caesar's." He answered them, "Render then the things that are Caesar's to Caesar and the things that are God's to God." He defeated them in their plot (vv. 18-22).

c. By the Sadducees

The Sadducees were the modernists at their time in the Jewish religion, not believing in the resurrection. Today among Christians there are modernists. They do not believe in the Bible or in the birth of Christ by a virgin. They do not believe that Christ died on the cross for our sins but that He died on the cross merely as a martyr. They do not believe in the resurrection or in miracles. The modernists explain away all the miracles in the Bible. Those ancient Sadducees were the ancient modernists.

They tempted the first God-man by telling Him that among them there were seven brothers who married one woman consecutively. Then they asked Him whose wife this woman would be in the resurrection. He said that they erred and did not know the Scriptures nor the power of God, for in the resurrection they neither marry nor are given in marriage, but are like angels in heaven. He taught them that God as the God of Abraham, the God of Isaac, and the God of Jacob is not the God of the dead, but of the living.

God is the God of the living, but Abraham, Isaac, and Jacob were dead. How could God be their God? Since God is called the God of these three dead persons, this indicates they will be resurrected. Without the interpretation of the Lord Jesus, we could not see the light that this divine title indicates resurrection. This is why the Lord told the Sadducees that they did not know the Scripture. They knew it in its words but not in its intrinsic significance. By this He muzzled their mouths (vv. 23-34).

d. By a Lawyer of the Pharisees

A lawyer of the Pharisees, knowing that the first God-man muzzled the mouths of the Sadducees, tested Him by asking Him which is the great commandment in the law (vv. 34-36).

He answered, " 'You shall love the Lord your God with all your heart and with all your soul and with all your mind.' This is the great and first commandment. And the second is like it: 'You shall love your neighbor as yourself.' On these two commandments hang all the Law and the Prophets." By this He conquered them also (vv. 37-40).

e. The First God-man Turning the Test to Them

All those who tested the Lord were defeated, muzzled. Actually, He was the only one qualified to test. He tested them by saying, "What do you think concerning the Christ? Whose son is He?" Their questions indicated that they were concerned about Roman imperialism, their Jewish belief, and their creed (the law). The Lord indicated that those things meant nothing. What mattered was Christ. He is what they needed. When He asked them whose son Christ is, they answered, "David's." He said, "How then does David in spirit call Him Lord [Psa. 110:1]...? If then David calls Him Lord, how is He his son?" (vv. 41-45). Not one of them was able to answer Him a word, nor did anyone from that day dare to question Him anymore (v. 46).

The Pharisees, the Herodians, the Sadducees, and a lawyer of the Pharisees tempted the first God-man with questions concerning Roman imperialism, the belief of the Jewish religion, and their creed, thinking that they could ensnare Him, but He defeated them all by His wise and subduing answers, which led them to consider the person of Christ who, not the political and religious things, was their real need. It was as if the Lord were saying, "You have to consider your real need. The real need for your life is Christ. But regretfully you don't know Him. You know Roman imperialism, Jewish belief, and the Jewish creed. You know all the political and religious things, but you don't know the very Christ who is your real need."

When He tested them with the person of Christ, they did not have the adequate knowledge, knowing Christ only in His humanity as the seed of David but not in His divinity as the Lord of David who will sit at the right hand of God (Psa.

110:1). Eventually, He muzzled all their mouths and won the victory in the mutual testings.

3. At the End of His Ministry

Now we want to consider the temptations through which the Lord passed at the end of His ministry (Matt. 26:57-68). This was at the time of His being judged by the Jewish Sanhedrin after He was arrested by the Roman authorities in the night (vv. 57-58). They tested Him about several things so that they might put Him to death, but He answered nothing (vv. 59-62). Eventually, the high priest tested Him concerning whether He was the Christ, the Son of God (v. 63). He answered, "You have said rightly. Nevertheless I say to you, From now on you will see the Son of Man sitting at the right hand of Power [Psa. 110:1] and coming on the clouds of heaven" (v. 64). The Lord Jesus referred them to Psalm 110:1, which says, "Jehovah saith unto my Lord, Sit thou at my right hand, / Until I make thine enemies thy footstool" (ASV). Although He was a man, He could sit at the right hand of God. He was saying that He was equal to God, and that offended the Jews, but it was prophesied by David in Psalm 110:1. He also said that the Son of Man would come on the clouds of heaven. This word has not yet been fulfilled. We believe that the Lord Jesus as the Son of Man will come on the clouds of heaven to take the earth and possess it (Rev. 10:1-2).

When the high priest heard this man, Jesus of Nazareth, say that He would sit at the right hand of God, making Himself equal with God, the high priest tore his garments and said that He had blasphemed, and the Sanhedrin considered that He was worthy of death (Matt. 26:65-66). They spit in His face and beat Him with their fists, and others slapped Him (vv. 67-68).

In the last temptation of the first God-man by the high priest usurped by Satan, the high priest's test was in principle the same as the devil's in the beginning of the temptations, tempting the first God-man to assume His divine position as the Son of God and ignore His human position as a man (Matt. 4:3-7). At the beginning Satan himself was tempting

the Lord. At the ending the high priest was tempting Him.
These two temptations were actually the same because the
high priest was usurped by Satan. His temptation was just
a repetition of that by Satan. They tempted the Lord to
assume His God-given position, the position of His divinity,
and ignore His God-ordained position, the position of humanity. The first God-man, knowing the stratagem of Satan, in
His answer again did not explicitly assume His divine position
as the Son of God but strongly stressed His human position
as the Son of Man to shame Satan and annul him by His
humanity. The Lord's standing on the position of humanity
was a strong weapon for Him to defeat Satan and the
instrument usurped by Satan.

4. A Vivid Picture of the First God-man

In conclusion, all the temptations by Satan and his
usurped instruments present us a vivid picture that the first
God-man behaved stately within the limit of His positions
according to His dual status of God and man. His wisdom,
His honesty, His faithfulness to God, His sobermindedness
concerning His position and status, and His conquering and
subduing ability, all were shown in this ugly portrait of His
enemy Satan, the devil. The actual result of the temptations
by the opposers of the first God-man did afford a chance for
Him to unveil to them the person of Christ in full, that He
is both God as the Lord of David, their respected father, and
man, a seed of David, who will sit at the right hand of God
(Psa. 110:1). Such an all-inclusive Christ was the real need
for their life, but what a pity that they were blinded by Satan
and became ignorant of their real need so that they despised
Him, forsook Him, and sentenced Him to death by crucifixion!
(Matt. 26:66-67).

THE GOD-MAN LIVING

THE FIRST GOD-MAN'S LIVING
FROM THE MANGER TO THE CROSS

(4)

Scripture Reading: Phil. 2:8; Matt. 11:28-29; 12:16, 19-20; 9:36; 11:5; Luke 4:18-22; John 11:35; Luke 9:58, 53-56; Isa. 53:3, 7; 1 Pet. 4:1; 2:21-23; Luke 23:34a, 42-43; Heb. 2:18; 4:15; John 5:19, 30; 8:28; 14:10; 6:38; Matt. 26:39, 42; John 7:6, 8; 1 Tim. 3:16a

OUTLINE

IV. In His ministry:

  C. His living for His ministry:

    1. Based upon the significance of the water baptism:

      a. Realizing that a man in the flesh is good for nothing but death and burial.

      b. Denying His self and His natural man.

      c. Putting His self on the cross and living under the shadow of the cross all the time.

      d. Living a humble life by humbling Himself— Phil. 2:8.

      e. Living under the yoke of God, being meek and lowly in heart—Matt. 11:28-29.

      f. Charging people not to make Him known— Matt. 12:16.

      g. Not striving nor crying out nor making anyone hear His voice in the streets; a bruised reed He will not break, and smoking flax He will not quench until He brings forth justice unto victory—Matt. 12:19-20.

   h. Having a concern for God's flock—Matt. 9:36:

     1) Doing miracles to take care of the needy ones:

      "The blind receive their sight and the lame walk; the lepers are cleansed and the deaf hear; and the dead are raised and the poor have the gospel announced to them"—Matt. 11:5.

     2) Preaching the gospel to the poor with words of grace proceeding out of His mouth—Luke 4:18-22.

     3) Sympathizing with the suffering and ignorant disciples, even unto weeping— John 11:35.

   i. Having not a place where He may lay His head, though the foxes have holes, and the birds of heaven have roosts—Luke 9:58.

   j. Correcting His disciples to have a right spirit toward the rejecting ones—Luke 9:53-56.

   k. Suffering afflictions without avenging, leaving us a model so that we may follow in His steps—Isa. 53:3, 7; 1 Pet. 4:1; 2:21-23.

   l. In His crucifixion He prayed for those who were crucifying Him, that the Father would forgive them their sin of ignorance—Luke 23:34a.

   m. Even in His suffering and dying He extended His salvation to one of the criminals who were crucified with Him—Luke 23:42-43.

   n. Being tempted but without sin—Heb. 2:18; 4:15; 1 Pet. 2:22.

   o. Doing nothing from Himself—John 5:19, 30a; 8:28.

   p. Not speaking any word from Himself—John 14:10a.

   q. Not seeking His own will but the will of God—John 5:30b; 6:38; Matt. 26:39, 42:

     "My Father, if it is possible, let this cup pass

from Me; yet not as I will, but as You will."
"My Father, if this cannot pass away unless
I drink it, Your will be done."

   r. Being obedient to God even unto death, and
that the death of a cross—Phil. 2:8.

2. Having no freedom to live according to Himself:

   a. He said to His brothers, "My time has not
yet come, but your time is always ready"—
John 7:6.

   b. "You go up to the feast; I am not going up
to this feast, because My time has not yet
been fulfilled"—v. 8.

3. Coordinating with the Father who abides and
works in Him for the accomplishment of His
economy—John 14:10b.

4. Manifesting God to express God's attributes in
His human virtues—1 Tim. 3:16a.

C. His Living for His Ministry

Thus far, we have seen the first God-man's living in His infancy, in His youth, and in His silence between the age of twelve and the age of thirty. We have also seen His living in the commencement of His ministry and in His temptations. In this message we want to see the first God-man's living for His ministry. We need to consider our living for our ministry. Many people today are living on this earth with no purpose. I came to the United States to live a life for my ministry. If it were not for the ministry, I would not have come to this country. We are living for the Lord's ministry.

1. Based upon the Significance of Water Baptism

a. Realizing That a Man in the Flesh Is Good for Nothing but Death and Burial

When He commenced His ministry, before He did anything, He came to John to be baptized. Water baptism signifies that a man in the flesh in the eyes of God is good for nothing but death and burial. Christ's living for His ministry was based upon this significance of water baptism. We need to have the same base in our living.

b. Denying His Self and His Natural Man

Based upon this significance, Christ denied His self and His natural man. We should not forget what our water baptism means to us. It means that we were buried. We should not deal with our spouse the way that we did in the past. Based upon our having been buried, we should deny our self and our natural man. We should not do anything by our natural life, because it has been buried.

c. Putting His Self on the Cross

The Lord put His self on the cross and lived under the shadow of the cross all the time. He said, "If anyone wants to come after Me, let him deny himself and take up his cross and follow Me" (Matt. 16:24). We followers of Christ should apply the cross to our self all the time. We should continuously live under the shadow of the cross. Throughout my entire

Christian life, I have been learning the lessons of putting my self on the cross and of living under the shadow of the cross. From the very beginning of my following the Lord, I was taught to follow Him by bearing the cross. It does not matter whether our natural man is good or bad. We should reject and deny our natural man, even if it is good. We should not think that we should live by our natural life because it is meek, gentle, and good to people. We have to remember that that meek, gentle life was buried when we were baptized. Our life today is Christ as the Spirit, the divine life.

d. Living a Humble Life

Christ also lived a humble life by humbling Himself (Phil. 2:8). This shows that we should not be proud of anything. We have nothing that is worth being proud about. Paul was given a thorn in the flesh because God was concerned that he would be proud because of the revelations he had seen. God allowed a thorn to be placed upon him to subdue him from being proud.

e. Living under the Yoke of God

In His earthly ministry the Lord also lived under the yoke of God, being meek and lowly in heart (Matt. 11:28-29). For our ministry's sake, we should be living such a life under the yoke. An animal under the yoke must labor to plow the land under the master's direction. When we are under the yoke of God, we have no freedom, no choice, no preference.

f. Charging People Not to Make Him Known

Matthew 12:16 says that the Lord charged people not to make Him known. This means that He did not want to be renowned. All the co-workers are facing such a temptation. Some like to be renowned, to be known by everybody, but the Lord Jesus was contrary to this. To be popular is a temptation. When we want to be popular, we are finished. Some Christian workers dare not say anything bad about people, because they want to be popular. They will not say certain things out of fear that they will not be invited the next time. In 1964 I was invited to speak to a group of believers in Dallas. I was welcomed by them because I ministered Christ to them. Eventually, at the end of my time with them, I spoke about the church being the Body of Christ. I was rejected because of this. We must be faithful to speak the truths of the divine revelation. One former co-worker dared not say that Christ as the last Adam became a life-giving Spirit, because he said this would offend others. This is contrary to the living of the first God-man. He was not seeking to be accepted by everyone to make a name for Himself.

g. Not Striving nor Crying Out nor Making Anyone Hear His Voice in the Streets

Matthew 12:19 and 20 say, "He will not strive nor cry out, nor will anyone hear His voice in the streets. A bruised reed He will not break, and smoking flax He will not quench until He brings forth justice unto victory." In ancient times the Jews made flutes of reeds. When a reed was bruised, they broke it. Also, they made torches out of flax, which can burn oil. When the oil ran out, the flax smoked and they quenched it. Some of the Lord's people are like a bruised reed, which cannot give a musical sound; others are like smoking flax, which cannot produce a shining light. Yet the Lord will not break the bruised ones or quench the smoking ones. Some of those who are as bruised reeds and smoking flax will be used by Christ to bring forth justice unto victory. If we think that no one is useful except ourself, we cannot carry out the Lord's work. When we select co-workers, we may consider only how they appear outwardly, but they may not be that faithful. The Lord would select some bruised reeds and smoking flax. Then He would perfect them so that they could become useful in His hand to bring forth justice unto victory. We should use what the Lord has given us. If He gives us good ones, we should use the good ones. If He gives us bad ones, we should use the bad ones.

h. Having a Concern for God's Flock

When the Lord saw the crowds, "He was moved with compassion for them, because they were harassed and cast away like sheep not having a shepherd" (Matt. 9:36). He did miracles to take care of the needy ones. He said, "The blind receive their sight and the lame walk; the lepers are cleansed and the deaf hear; and the dead are raised and the poor have the gospel announced to them" (11:5). This is the mercy exercised by the Lord as their Shepherd to take care of them. As a minister of the Lord, we should learn how to be concerned for the needy ones. The Lord also preached the gospel to the poor with words of grace proceeding out of His mouth (Luke 4:18-22). Sometimes we speak words of rebuking and condemnation instead of words of grace. We must learn to be one with the Lord to speak words of grace. Also, the Lord sympathized with the suffering and ignorant disciples, even unto weeping (John 11:35). Martha and Mary lost their brother Lazarus, but they still remained ignorant and that compelled the Lord to weep. The word *weep* here means "to weep silently." The Lord told them that Lazarus would be resurrected, but He was frustrated by human opinions. Martha postponed the resurrection to the last day (v. 24). Thus, the Lord Jesus wept. Many Christians today are suffering, without knowing why or what they should do under that suffering. The Lord sympathizes with this situation.

i. Having No Place to Lay His Head

The Lord did not have a place to lay His head, though the foxes have holes and the birds of heaven have roosts (Luke 9:58). We have to learn to suffer poverty in this way.

j. Correcting His Disciples to Have a Right Spirit

The Lord corrected His disciples to have a right spirit toward the rejecting ones. The Lord and His disciples passed a village which would not receive them. The two sons of thunder, James and John, asked, "Lord, do You want us to command fire to come down from heaven and consume them?" Then the Lord said, "You do not know of what kind of spirit you are" (Luke 9:53-56). This indicates that the Lord always treated people with a right spirit. I regretted that sometimes I had treated people with a wrong spirit. We must learn the lesson to correct our spirit in the way that we treat people. If we respond with a wrong spirit to people who do not receive us, we are not qualified to serve people. We cannot minister the word of God to people if we have a wrong spirit.

According to the New Testament, the church has only one local ground; there is only one church for one city. By practicing this we annul the standing of all the denominations. Because of this they would not receive or welcome us. Should we respond the way James and John did in Luke 9, with a wrong spirit? We must exercise to have a right spirit. The Lord is a real model of the God-man living.

k. Suffering Afflictions without Avenging

The Lord suffered afflictions without avenging, leaving us a model so that we may follow in His steps (Isa. 53:3, 7; 1 Pet. 4:1; 2:21-23). He was suffering silently like a sheep before its shearers. When He was reviled, He did not revile in return. Today we co-workers must learn of this model. If people revile us, we should not have any thought of avenging by reviling them in return.

The Greek word for *model* literally means "a writing copy, an underwriting, used by students to trace letters and thereby learn to draw them." The Lord has set His suffering life before us so that we can copy it by tracing and following His steps. This does not refer to a mere imitation of Him and His life but to a reproduction of Him that comes from enjoying Him as grace in our sufferings, so that He Himself as the indwelling Spirit, with all the riches of His life, reproduces Himself in us. We become the reproduction of the original writing copy, not a mere imitation of Him produced by taking Him as our outward model.

l. Praying for Those Who Were Crucifying Him

In His crucifixion He prayed for those who were crucifying Him, that the Father would forgive them their sin of ignorance (Luke 23:34a).

m. Extending His Salvation to One of the Criminals

Even in His suffering and dying, He extended His salvation to one of the criminals who were crucified with Him (23:42-43).

n. Being Tempted but without Sin

Although Christ was tempted, He was without sin (Heb. 2:18; 4:15; 1 Pet. 2:22).

o. Doing Nothing from Himself

The Lord said that He did nothing from Himself (John 5:19, 30a; 8:28). This is because He considered Himself a buried person.

p. Not Speaking Any Word from Himself

The Lord did not speak His own words. He spoke the Father's words (John 14:10a).

q. Not Seeking His Own Will but the Will of God

He did not seek His own will but the will of God (John 5:30b; 6:38). In Matthew 26:39 He said, "My Father, if it is possible, let this cup pass from Me; yet not as I will, but as You will." Then in verse 42 He said, "My Father, if this cannot pass away unless I drink it, Your will be done."

r. Being Obedient to God Even unto Death

Philippians 2:8 says that the Lord was obedient unto death, and that the death of a cross.

2. Having No Freedom to Live according to Himself

The Lord had no freedom to live according to Himself. He said to His brothers, "My time has not yet come, but your time is always ready" (John 7:6). In verse 8 the Lord said, "You go up to the feast; I am not going up to this feast, because My time has not yet been fulfilled." The Lord lived on earth as a man, being limited even in the matter of time. This shows that before doing anything, we need to contact the Lord. We may pray, "Lord, I have a burden to go and see a certain brother. Is this the right time?" Often when I prayed in this way, the Lord told me that I should wait. I had a burden to help a brother, but the Lord would not allow me to do it then. We must learn the lesson of timing. We must learn not to act according to our preference.

Stanza 1 of *Hymns,* #501 says concerning Christ: "God infinite, in eternity, / Yet man in time, finite to be." He was God in eternity without limitation, but He became a man on this earth limited by time and space. He was limited to the village of Nazareth in His living for about thirty years. Can we be limited in such a way? We may have the burden to visit many places, but the Lord may not want us to. We must learn the lesson to be limited.

3. Coordinating with the Father

Everything that the Lord Jesus did was in coordination with the Father who abode and worked in Him for the accomplishment of His economy. In John 14:10b the Lord said, "The words that I say to you I do not speak from Myself, but the Father who abides in Me does His works." This was a coordination with the Father who lived and worked in Him.

4. Manifesting God to Express God's Attributes in His Human Virtues

He was on this earth living a life totally for the manifestation of God to express God's attributes in His human virtues (1 Tim. 3:16a). When people saw His virtues, they saw God's attributes, and that was a manifestation of God. We need to apply all of these points to our daily living in our contact with everyone.

THE GOD-MAN LIVING

MESSAGE NINE

THE FIRST GOD-MAN'S LIVING
FROM THE MANGER TO THE CROSS

(5)

Scripture Reading: Matt. 3:16; Heb. 1:9; Acts 10:38a; Luke 4:18-19; Matt. 12:18a; 4:1-2; Luke 4:1; John 3:34; Acts 10:38b; Matt. 12:18b, 28; Rev. 1:5; 3:14; 1 Tim. 3:16; Heb. 9:14

OUTLINE

IV. In His ministry:
  D. His moving for His ministry:
    1. Under the Spirit's anointing:
      a. After He was baptized in the water, God anointed Him with the Spirit descending upon Him as a dove—Matt. 3:16.
      b. Anointed by God with the oil of exultant joy above His partners—Heb. 1:9.
      c. Anointed by God with the Holy Spirit and with power—Acts 10:38a.
      d. The Spirit of the Lord was upon Him—Luke 4:18a.
      e. God had put His Spirit upon Him—Matt. 12:18a.
      f. Led by the Holy Spirit to be tempted by the devil for forty days—Matt. 4:1-2; Luke 4:1.
      g. As the One sent by God, speaking the words of God and giving the Spirit not by measure—John 3:34.
      h. Going about doing good and healing all those who were being oppressed by the devil—Acts 10:38b.

     i. Announcing the gospel to the poor, proclaiming release to the captives, and recovery of sight to the blind, and sending away in release those who are oppressed—Luke 4:18-19.

     j. Announcing justice to the Gentiles—Matt. 12:18b.

     k. By the Spirit of God casting out the demons for the coming of the kingdom of God—Matt. 12:28.

     l. Witnessing God faithfully—Rev. 1:5; 3:14.

    m. Justified in the Spirit—1 Tim. 3:16.

    n. Through the eternal Spirit offering Himself without blemish to God that He may purify our conscience with His blood from dead works to serve the living God—Heb. 9:14.

2. That the God-man as God's anointed One, Messiah, Christ, moved under the anointing of the Spirit of God is the accomplishment of God's eternal economy in the God-man's ministry while He was in the flesh and on the earth.

3. Christ as the first God-man on the one hand lived by the Father, who abode and worked in Him, and on the other hand moved and ministered by the Spirit. This indicates that the living of the first God-man was actually the living and moving of the processed Triune God in Christ's human living on the earth.

D. His Moving for His Ministry

Now that we have seen the living of Christ for His ministry, we want to go on to see His moving for His ministry. His living for the ministry is concerning His life. His moving for His ministry is concerning His work. The cross was the center of Christ's living. The Spirit was the center of His work. The cross came first, and then the Spirit.

1. Under the Spirit's Anointing

Christ's move in His work was altogether under the Spirit's anointing.

a. God's Anointing Him with the Spirit

After He was baptized in the water, God anointed Him with the Spirit descending upon Him as a dove (Matt. 3:16). His being baptized signifies that He took the cross to put the man of flesh to death for burial. After the cross, God anointed Him with the Spirit. This shows us the operation of the Divine Trinity. The Father anointed the Son with the Spirit descending upon Him as a gentle and meek dove. This anointing was to equip Christ for His work and to armor Christ for His fighting. The weapon for Christ's fighting is not a bomb but a dove. Also, the instrument for His work is not an ax but a dove. Today we are fighting for the kingdom of God and working for Christ, but we must remember that a dove is both our weapon and our instrument. Christ was a dove as He was being arrested and as He was being judged before the Jewish Sanhedrin. He was a dove before Pilate and Herod, the Roman authorities. He fought with and worked with a dove. Today we are fighting, working, laboring, and struggling, but our weapon and our instrument should be a dove. A dove has two eyes but it can see only one thing at a time. This means that we should have a single view, focusing on God to trust in Him continually.

b. Anointed by God with the Oil of Exultant Joy

Christ was anointed by God with the oil of exultant joy above His partners (Heb. 1:9). If you have God's anointing, you will be exultantly joyful. He was anointed with the oil of exultant joy above His partners. We cannot compare with Him. Even Peter and Paul cannot compare with Him. He is above all of us in this matter of anointing.

c. Anointed by God with the Holy Spirit and with Power

Acts 10:38a says that God anointed Jesus with the Holy Spirit and with power. Today the Spirit of God is so powerful. No one can measure His power to subdue the whole earth.

d. The Spirit of the Lord Being upon Him

In Luke 4:18a the Lord said that the Spirit of the Lord was upon Him.

e. God Having Put His Spirit upon Him

In Matthew 12:18a God said concerning Christ, "I will put My Spirit upon Him." God put such a powerful Spirit upon Christ in the flesh on the earth—a gentle, meek, and humble man.

f. Led by the Holy Spirit

He was not only under but also led by the Holy Spirit to be tempted by the devil for forty days (Matt. 4:1-2; Luke 4:1). In the universe, only the devil can have a kind of transaction with God as His opponent. God sent His Son to be a man with the intention to defeat Satan, but the Spirit of God led this One to be tempted by Satan. This was a kind of a test for forty days. Every chosen slave, or servant, of God through the centuries has been firstly tested by the devil. We should not think that if we answer God's call, we will be prosperous. The first thing we meet will not be prosperity but testing. Testing is not sweet but a difficult thing. We cannot escape. We have to pass the test.

g. Speaking the Words of God and Giving the Spirit Not by Measure

As the One sent by God, Christ spoke the words of God and gave the Spirit not by measure (John 3:34). The Spirit was given by God to Him, and He gives the Spirit not by measure. The Spirit dwells within us unlimitedly. Christ is the One who speaks the word with the Spirit. When He speaks the word of God, He gives the Spirit without measure. When we speak the word, we should minister, dispense, the Spirit. Without the dispensing of the Spirit, our word is vanity and also death. Without the giving of the Spirit to accompany the speaking of the word, the word spoken by us is dead letters. We may hear just one message, but the Spirit we receive of the Lord in this message by His speaking is not by measure. To come to the meeting to hear the word is not vain. When we hear the word of God, the Spirit of God goes along with this word not by measure. We may hear only one message, but the measure of the Spirit we receive is without limitation.

h. Going About Doing Good and Healing
All Those Who Were Being Oppressed by the Devil

He defeated the devil in the devil's temptation. From that time onward, He was going about to do good and to heal all those who were being oppressed by the devil (Acts 10:38b). He defeated the devil first; then He went out to defeat the devil for the release of the oppressed ones.

i. Announcing the Gospel to the Poor

Christ announced the gospel to the poor, proclaiming release to the captives, and recovery of sight to the blind, and sending away in release those who are oppressed (Luke 4:18-19).

j. Announcing Justice to the Gentiles

Matthew 12:18b says that He announced justice to the Gentiles. *Justice* here refers to the all-inclusive Christ. If you have Christ, you have justice and peace. With injustice there is no peace and satisfaction. The nations of the world are struggling and fighting against one another because of injustice. None of them is satisfied. Justice means Christ is satisfying you. When we have Christ, we are satisfied, and our conflict with others is terminated. When we are announcing Christ as everything to people, Christ satisfies them and brings them justice. If there is a feeling of injustice between you and someone else, this indicates you are short of Christ. You need to receive more of Christ; then justice is there.

k. Casting Out Demons by the Spirit of God

By the Spirit of God, Christ cast out demons for the coming of the kingdom of God (Matt. 12:28).

l. Witnessing God Faithfully

Revelation 1:5 and 3:14 say that Christ is the faithful Witness. His expressing God was His witnessing. Many people wondered who He was. This man was God, witnessing God.

m. Justified in the Spirit

First Timothy 3:16 says that He was justified in the Spirit. He was opposed, persecuted, and rejected by man, but He was justified in the Spirit. As One who was in the Spirit, He could not be condemned or criticized by anyone.

n. Through the Eternal Spirit, He Offered Himself without Blemish to God

Through the eternal Spirit, He offered Himself without blemish to God that He may purify our conscience with His blood from dead works to serve the living God (Heb. 9:14). For Christ to offer Himself to God to be crucified to accomplish redemption to bring us back to serve the living God was a great thing. This was difficult for Him in His humanity as seen by His prayer at Gethsemane. He prayed three times for the Father, if possible, to remove the cup of death from Him, but He ended by praying, "Yet not as I will, but as You will" (Matt. 26:39-44). That indicates that even He, Christ in the flesh, was suffering something that was not so easy for His humanity. He realized the need of the strengthening of the Spirit, so He offered Himself, including His humanity, to God through the eternal Spirit. What He accomplished in His redemption was eternal, because that was done through the eternal Spirit. This indicates that He did everything through the Spirit.

2. The Accomplishment of God's Eternal Economy in the God-man's Ministry

The God-man as God's anointed One, Messiah, Christ, moved under the anointing of the Spirit of God. This was the accomplishment of God's eternal economy in the God-man's ministry while He was in the flesh and on the earth.

3. Living by the Father and Moving by the Spirit

Christ as the first God-man on the one hand lived by the Father, who abode and worked in Him (John 14:10), and on the other hand moved and ministered by the Spirit. John 14:10 says, "Do you not believe that I am in the Father and the Father is in Me? The words that I say to you I do not speak from Myself, but the Father who abides in Me does His works." This proves that while Christ was working, the Father was working in Him by abiding in Him. His living by the Father and ministering by the Spirit indicate that the living of the first God-man was actually the living and moving of the processed Triune God in Christ's human living on the earth.

THE GOD-MAN LIVING

MESSAGE TEN

THE FIRST GOD-MAN'S LIVING
A MAN OF PRAYER

(1)

Scripture Reading: Phil. 3:12-14, 8; John 10:30; Acts 10:38c; John 8:29; 16:32; 1 Pet. 2:23b; Luke 23:46; John 14:30b; Matt. 3:13—4:11; 6:5, 16; 17:21; Acts 13:2-3

OUTLINE

I. A man of prayer:
  A. Not as a common man praying common prayers to God.
  B. Not as a pious man, a so-called godly man, praying to God in a religious way.
  C. Not as a God-seeking man praying to God for the divine attainments and obtainments.
  D. Not even as merely a Christ-seeker praying desperately to gain Christ in His excellency—Phil. 3:12-14, 8.
  E. But a man in the flesh praying to the mysterious God in the divine, mystical realm, and a man who is:
    1. One with God—John 10:30.
    2. Living in the presence of God without ceasing—Acts 10:38c; John 8:29; 16:32.
    3. Trusting in God and not in Himself, under any kind of suffering and persecution—1 Pet. 2:23b; Luke 23:46.
    4. And in whom Satan, the ruler of the world, had nothing (no ground, no chance, no hope, no possibility in anything)—John 14:30b.
II. The divine facts in the mystical human life of the

first God-man in the record of the synoptic Gospels
concerning the first God-man as the King-Savior in
the kingdom of the heavens, the Slave-Savior in God's
gospel service, and the Man-Savior in God's salvation:
A. After His baptism in the water, and God's anointing from the heavens with the great commission
   for Him to bring in the kingdom of the heavens
   to the earth, He, under the leading of the Spirit,
   went to the wilderness to fast forty days and forty
   nights—Matt. 3:13—4:11:
   1. He should have felt that:
      a. His Father's divine commission to Him
         concerning the kingdom of the heavens was
         a great and critical burden to Him.
      b. He needed to seek His Father's counsel
         concerning how to bring His Father's king-
         dom in the heavens to the fallen Adamic
         race on the earth.
   2. According to the common practice of fasting, it
      is always accompanied by prayer—Matt. 6:5,
      16; 17:21; Acts 13:2-3.
   3. But there is no mention of prayer accompanying
      the first God-man's fasting, not only in forty
      days but also in forty nights.
   4. We should believe that there should have been
      such an accompanying prayer, but it is kept in
      secret as a mystery and it is impossible for us
      to know what the content was.
   5. This indicates that the first God-man's prayer
      was in the divine, mystical realm.

In this message we want to continue our fellowship on the first God-man's living by seeing Him as a man of prayer.

I. A MAN OF PRAYER

The Lord lived as a man of prayer. He did not live as a common man praying common prayers to God, as a pious man, a so-called godly man, praying to God in a religious way, or as a God-seeking man praying to God for the divine attainments and obtainments. His being a man of prayer was not even as merely a Christ-seeker praying desperately to gain Christ in His excellency (Phil. 3:12-14, 8). Instead, He was a man in the flesh praying to the mysterious God in the divine, mystical realm. The Gospels tell us that He often went to the mountain or withdrew to a private place to pray (Matt. 14:23; Mark 1:35; Luke 5:16; 6:12; 9:28).

According to what I have learned, we may be a Christ-seeker, praying desperately to gain Christ in His excellency, yet this is not the pure pattern of the man of prayer revealed in the Gospels. If we are a Christ-seeker, we would think that we are very special and spiritual. But in describing the first God-man as a man of prayer, I have avoided using the word *spiritual*. Instead, I have used the words *divine* and *mystical*. *Divine* is on God's side. *Mystical* is on man's side. On the one hand, Jesus was a man in the flesh, yet He prayed to the mysterious God in the divine and mystical way and realm.

He was a man of prayer, a man who is one with God (John 10:30). We may be a Christ-seeker, desperately praying to gain Christ, yet we may not be one with God. He was also a man living in the presence of God without ceasing (Acts 10:38c; John 8:29; 16:32). He told us that He was never alone, but the Father was with Him. Every moment He saw His Father's face. We may seek Christ, yet not live in the presence of God so closely and continuously without ceasing. Also, He trusted in God and not in Himself, under any kind of suffering and persecution. First Peter 2:23b says that in the midst of His suffering He did not speak threatening words but kept committing all to Him who judges righteously. Luke 23:46 says that at the time He was dying on the cross, He prayed,

"Father, into Your hands I commit My spirit." In our daily life, do we trust in God when trouble comes? Maybe we do to a small extent, but not absolutely.

In John 14:30 the Lord said, "The ruler of the world is coming, and in Me he has nothing." This means that in the Lord Jesus, Satan as the ruler of the world had no ground, no chance, no hope, no possibility in anything. If we are enlightened, we will admit that Satan has too many things in us. He has the ground, the chance, the hope, and the possibility in many things. But here is a man of prayer who said that Satan, the ruler of the world, had nothing in Him. This is a particular sentence in the whole Bible. Thus, Christ was a man of prayer, a man who is one with God, lives in the presence of God continuously, trusts in God in His suffering and persecution, and in whom Satan has nothing.

II. THE DIVINE FACTS IN THE MYSTICAL HUMAN LIFE OF THE FIRST GOD-MAN

All of the Lord's prayers are divine facts. We need to ask if our prayers are divine facts. A wife may ask the Lord to take care of her family because her husband has lost his job. Such a prayer is not divine. Instead, she may pray, "Lord, as a housewife, I praise You and thank You that we are in Your hands. We trust in You in this circumstance." This is divine prayer. If we pray, "Lord, today there is a need for people to go to Moscow," this is not divine prayer. Instead, we should pray, "Lord, thank You that You are now spreading Your recovery to Russia. Lord, this is Your move." This is divine prayer.

When we consider the Lord's prayer in John 17, we can see what divine prayer is. We may pray for our need, but we have to pray about it in a divine way. We should pray divine prayers, not human prayers. All the prayers Christ prayed were divine facts in His mystical human life. Although we are human, people should sense that there is something mystical about us. Our classmates, colleagues, or peers should sense that there is something about us that they cannot understand. This is because we are mysterious, mystical. The

One who prayed the prayer recorded in John 17 was Jesus of Nazareth, a man in the flesh, yet His prayer was mystical.

A sister who lost her son once said she could not understand why it was that the more she loved the Lord, the more she seemed to lose. She prayed, "Lord, don't You know I love You? Why did You take away my son?" This is not only a human prayer but also a fleshly prayer. Based upon this light, we should consider our prayers. We pray many human and fleshly prayers, not divine prayers. No prayer is as high as the Lord's prayer in John 17. He prayed, "Father, the hour has come; glorify Your Son that the Son may glorify You" (v. 1). Christ's prayer is divine. When He was dying on the cross, He prayed, "Father, forgive them, for they do not know what they are doing" (Luke 23:34). He prayed to the Father for the forgiveness of His crucifiers. That was divine and mystical.

We want to see the divine facts in the mystical human life of the first God-man in the record of the synoptic Gospels. After His baptism in the water and God's anointing from the heavens with the great commission for Him to bring in the kingdom of the heavens to the earth, He, under the leading of the Spirit, went to the wilderness to fast for forty days and forty nights (Matt. 3:13—4:11). He should have felt that His Father's divine commission to Him concerning the kingdom of the heavens was a great and critical burden to Him. He needed to seek His Father's counsel concerning how to bring His Father's kingdom in the heavens to the fallen Adamic race on the earth. According to the common practice of fasting, it is always accompanied by prayer (Matt. 6:5, 16; 17:21; Acts 13:2-3). But there is no mention of prayer accompanying the first God-man's fasting, not only in forty days but also in forty nights. The Lord's prayer which obviously accompanied His long period of fasting is not recorded. This is very meaningful. We should believe that there was such an accompanying prayer, but it is kept in secret as a mystery and it is impossible for us to know what the content was. This indicates that the first God-man's prayer was in the divine, mystical realm.

The pattern of the first God-man being a man of prayer

shows that we should do everything in a divine way. Even a husband's loving his wife should be divine and not human. Our buying a pair of shoes and the way that we cut our hair should be divine. A very critical part of the history of the first God-man was His prayer. All of His prayers were divine, yet they were in a human life, making that human life mystical. He lived a mystical human life. A husband should love his wife divinely, not merely spiritually. This is because he does not love her in his way but in God's way and not with his love but with God's love. How could a man in the flesh love his wife in a divine way and with the divine love? This is mystical. We should be persons living a life which is divine yet mystical. Our life should be divine yet human—not merely human, but mystically human. This is what is unveiled in the holy Word.

We have a concept concerning spirituality which blinds us. We need to see that we should not be merely spiritual but divine and mystical. Every believer today should be a divine and a mystical person. We should be divine yet so mysterious. Even those who are close to us should be able to sense that there is something about us which is mysterious and cannot be understood. The key is that although we are human, we live divinely. True spirituality should make us divine. This is higher.

Sometimes when we hear a young sister giving a testimony, we have the sense that her speaking is divine yet mystical. Everything in our living should be divine and mystical. This is what we see in the Lord Jesus. When people saw what He did, they were astounded and said, "Where did this man get this wisdom and these works of power? Is not this the carpenter's son?" (Matt. 13:54-55). This is because all that He did was divine and mystical. God was living through Him. He was God manifested in the flesh. This is a great mystery. First Timothy 3:16 says that the great mystery of godliness is God manifested in the flesh. The divine is manifested in a mystical human way.

The title *God-man* indicates clearly that Jesus was a man, but He was living God. Today you are a God-man. This means that you are a man, yet you live God and express God. You are a man, yet it is God who lives in you. This is the significance of the title *God-man*. A God-man's living is a man living God.

THE GOD-MAN LIVING

MESSAGE ELEVEN

THE FIRST GOD-MAN'S LIVING
A MAN OF PRAYER

(2)

Scripture Reading: Matt. 6:5-18; 7:7-8

OUTLINE

II. The divine facts in the mystical human life of the first God-man in the record of the synoptic Gospels concerning the first God-man as the King-Savior in the kingdom of the heavens, the Slave-Savior in God's gospel service, and the Man-Savior in God's salvation:

B. In His supreme teaching on the mount, the first God-man as the King-Savior in the kingdom of the heavens taught His disciples twice concerning prayer:

1. The first time is in the central part of His supreme teaching, unveiling to His disciples the heavenly vision concerning the prayer which is critical to the kingdom life, with four negative charges as warnings—Matt. 6:5-18:

a. The prayer: "Our Father who is in the heavens, Your name be sanctified; Your kingdom come; Your will be done, as in heaven, so also on earth. Give us today our daily bread. And forgive us our debts, as we also have forgiven our debtors. And do not bring us into temptation, but deliver us from the evil one. For Yours is the kingdom and the power and the glory forever. Amen" (vv. 9-13). This brief but critical prayer covers:

1) The Father's holy name to be sanctified.

2) The Father's heavenly kingdom to come.

3) The Father's divine will to be done on earth as in the heavens.

4) The care of the supply of our necessity, our daily bread.

5) The Father's forgiving of our debts as we have done with our debtors.

6) Not bringing us into temptation but delivering us from the devil, the evil one.

7) Recognizing and praising reverently that the kingdom, the power, and the glory belong to the Father forever.

Note: Such a critical prayer surely increases our seeking of the kingdom of the heavens as the Father's heart's desire and affords us our need of the divine supply of grace to fulfill all the supreme and strict requirements of the kingdom of the heavens for the Father's good pleasure.

b. The four negative charges as warnings—vv. 5-8, 14-18:

1) His disciples should not pray as the hypocrites do, loving to make a show publicly that they may be seen by men and receive glory from them according to the lust of their fleshly desire; the disciples should enter into their private room, shutting their door and praying to the Father in the heavens to be seen by Him in secret and repaid by Him—vv. 5-6.

2) Neither should they pray as the Gentiles do, babbling empty words, supposing that in their multiplicity of words they will be heard; the disciples should not do like them, for the Father of the disciples knows the things that they need before they ask Him—vv. 7-8.

3) If His disciples forgive men's offenses,

their heavenly Father will forgive the disciples also; otherwise, their Father will not forgive their offenses. This annuls their prayer to their heavenly Father— vv. 14-15.

4) His disciples should not fast like the sullen-faced hypocrites, disfiguring their faces that their fast may appear to men. The disciples should fast by anointing their head and washing their face that their fast may not appear to men but to their Father who is in secret and who sees it and will repay them—vv. 16-18.

2. The second time is in the conclusion of His supreme teaching concerning the kingdom of the heavens, when He promised the seekers of the kingdom of the heavens in Matthew 7:7-8, that they:

a. "Ask [indicating the prayer at a distance] and it shall be given to you."

b. "Seek [indicating the pursuit of what is prayed for] and you shall find."

c. "Knock [indicating the reaching of the goal of what is sought] and it shall be opened to you."

Note: Such a promise assures the seekers of the kingdom of the heavens that they will be given an open door to enter into all the blessings in the kingdom of the heavens.

We want to continue to see the divine facts in the mystical human life of the first God-man, who was a man of prayer. His mystical human life was a divine realm, and this realm is the kingdom of God. The genuine and proper prayer should always be divine, not just spiritual. This means that the Triune God prays with us and that we pray by living with the Triune God. He is indwelling us and is one with us. The New Testament reveals clearly that the consummated Spirit, the Spirit of God as the life-giving Spirit and the Spirit of Christ, indwells us (Rom. 8:2, 9-11). Second Timothy 4:22 says that the Lord is with our spirit. The consummated God today as the compound life-giving Spirit indwells us. We are human beings, no doubt, but the divine person was added to us.

For us to be spiritual is inadequate. We have to see that God has made Himself one with us and made us one with Him. Thus, each of us believers is a God-man. In this sense, we are God in life and in nature, but of course, not in His Godhead. This is because we have been born of Him to be of His species (John 1:12-13). We are one kind with Him. Based upon this revelation, we can see that genuine prayer should be the divine expression. If we pray by ourselves, that is the human expression. If we pray by living with God and moving with Christ, we pray from this Person and our prayers are divine. I feel that this is a new revelation to us in these days.

Only a divine person could pray, "Our Father who is in the heavens, Your name be sanctified" (Matt. 6:9). A divine, human person is a mystery. He is altogether mystical. There is a realm in this universe which is divine and mystical. The worldly people do not know this realm. They are in the physical, fallen, sinful, evil world. But we have been separated from being common; we have been sanctified and separated unto our God, who is holy. Now we are in the divine and mystical realm of the consummated Spirit.

B. In His Supreme Teaching on the Mount, the First God-man Teaching His Disciples Twice concerning Prayer

Matthew's record is concerning the first God-man as the King-Savior in the kingdom of the heavens. We have seen the

divine fact of His fasting in the wilderness for forty days and
forty nights. Now we want to see His supreme teaching on
the mount concerning prayer. Many Bible scholars call this
"the sermon on the mount," but I do not like the word *sermon*.
Instead, I use the term *supreme teaching*. No teaching in
human history is higher than this one. In His supreme
teaching on the mount, the first God-man as the King-Savior
in the kingdom of the heavens taught His disciples twice
concerning prayer. The first time is in the middle of the
supreme teaching, and the second time concludes His supreme
teaching.

1. The First Time Unveiling the Heavenly Vision concerning the Prayer Which Is Critical to the Kingdom Life

Many so-called churches today recite the prayer which the
Lord taught us to pray in Matthew 6 (vv. 5-18), but most do
not understand the real significance of what they are reciting.
This prayer is critical to the kingdom life, a life that lives in
the kingdom of the heavens. This one prayer also is
accompanied by four negative charges as warnings.

a. The Prayer

The prayer is as follows: "Our Father who is in the heavens,
Your name be sanctified; Your kingdom come; Your will be
done, as in heaven, so also on earth. Give us today our daily
bread. And forgive us our debts, as we also have forgiven our
debtors. And do not bring us into temptation, but deliver us
from the evil one. For Yours is the kingdom and the power
and the glory forever. Amen" (vv. 9-13). The praying ones
must be children of God, born of God, so they have the
authority, the right, to call God their Father. We cannot call
a person our father if we are not born of him. We have a
Father in the heavens who has begotten us. This brief but
critical prayer covers a number of crucial items.

1) The Father's Holy Name to Be Sanctified

To be sanctified means to be separated and distinct from
all that is common. On the fallen earth there are many false

gods. The worldly people consider our God as being in common with those gods. If we pray for our Father's name to be sanctified, we should not just utter this with our words. For His name to be sanctified, we should express Him in our living. We must live a sanctified life, a daily life separated from being common. To pray such a prayer needs us to be sanctified persons, those who are separated from being common. We should be distinct, separate, from all of the people around us. In other words, we should be holy. As sanctified people, we should pray, "Our Father, Your name be sanctified."

2) The Father's Heavenly Kingdom to Come

Today the world is not God's kingdom but His enemy's kingdom. This is why the Bible says that Satan is the ruler of today's world (John 12:31). In Satan's kingdom, the world, there is no righteousness, no peace, and no joy. Romans 14:17 tells us that the reality of the kingdom life is righteousness, peace, and joy in the Holy Spirit. In Satan's kingdom today, there is no joy, because there is no peace. In the United Nations, peace is talked about all the time, but there is no peace, because there is no righteousness. Peace is the issue of righteousness. In his second Epistle, Peter tells us that the unique thing that dwells in the new heavens and new earth is righteousness (3:13). In the coming kingdom, the millennium, the primary thing will be righteousness. There is no righteousness in today's world, because this is the kingdom of Satan, the evil ruler.

3) The Father's Divine Will to Be Done on Earth as in the Heavens

Today Satan's will is being done on the earth through evil men. Hitler, Mussolini, and Stalin tried to carry out his will along with most of the rulers on this earth today. Thank the Lord that Satan's will is not fully carried out. Hitler, Mussolini, and Stalin were destroyed. Napoleon wanted his will to be done, but he did not succeed. We need to pray for the Father's divine will to be done on earth as in the heavens. This is to bring the heavenly ruling, the kingdom of the heavens, to this earth. Then the Father's will surely will be done on the earth.

These three things—the name, the kingdom, and the will—are the attributes of the one Triune God. The name is of the Father, because the Father is the source; the kingdom is of the Son, and the will is of the Spirit. To pray in this way is to pray that the Triune God will be prevailing on the earth as He is prevailing in the heavens.

4) The Care of the Supply of Our Necessity, Our Daily Bread

In His prayer, the Lord covers our daily necessity. He teaches us to pray for our bread only for one day. We are to ask our Father to give us today, not tomorrow or next month, our daily bread. He does not want His people to worry about tomorrow. He wants them to pray only for today's needs. When I was younger, we co-workers in China sometimes came to the end of our material supply, and we did not know how we would live the next day. Something always came to meet our need for that day. The Lord is faithful to take care of the supply of our daily necessity.

5) The Father's Forgiving of Our Debts As We Have Done with Our Debtors

In the Lord's prayer, we see that we need to take care of our relationship with others. As we ask the Father to forgive us our debts, we should forgive our debtors. We are in debt with God, and we also have debtors who owe us something. To maintain a peaceful relationship with others, we have to forgive them. Thus, we have to clear up any separating factors between us and God and between us and others.

6) Not Bringing Us into Temptation but Delivering Us from the Devil, the Evil One

Sometimes our God, who is faithful and who takes care of us, brings us into a situation of temptation to test us as the Spirit of God did the Lord Jesus (Matt. 4:1). But because we know our weakness, we should pray, "Do not bring us into temptation." This indicates our knowledge of our weakness. To pray for deliverance from the evil one is to deal with Satan. The Lord's prayer takes care of the Triune God, of our daily necessity, of our relationship with God and with others, and also of Satan.

7) Recognizing and Praising Reverently That the Kingdom, the Power, and the Glory Belong to the Father Forever

The prayer to the Father concludes in this way: "For Yours is the kingdom and the power and the glory forever. Amen" (Matt. 6:13). Here is the realization and praise of God's kingdom, power, and glory. This also refers to the Triune God. The kingdom is of the Son, which is the realm in which God exercises His power. The power is of the Spirit, which carries out God's intention so that the Father can express His glory. This indicates that the prayer which the Lord teaches us to pray begins with the Triune God, in the sequence of the Father, the Son, and the Spirit, and ends also with the Triune God, but in the sequence of the Son, the Spirit, and the Father. Thus, the prayer taught by the Lord in His supreme teaching begins with God the Father and ends also with God the Father. God the Father is both the beginning and the end, the Alpha and the Omega.

Such a critical prayer surely increases our seeking of the kingdom of the heavens as the Father's heart's desire and affords us our need of the divine supply of grace to fulfill all the supreme and strict requirements of the kingdom of the heavens for the Father's good pleasure. On the one hand, we are seeking for something according to the Father's heart's desire. On the other hand, we have the supply to fulfill something for the Father's good pleasure.

b. The Four Negative Charges as Warnings

1) Not Praying As the Hypocrites Do

The Lord warned His disciples not to pray as the hypocrites do with a mask. They love to make a show publicly that they may be seen by men and receive glory from them according to the lust of their fleshly desire. Instead, the disciples should enter into their private room, shutting their door and praying to the Father in the heavens to be seen by Him in secret and repaid by Him (vv. 5-6). We have to learn to be secret persons. We should pray in our private place to be seen by the Father in secret, not by others for an outward public display. If we pray properly, God will repay us as a reward. The hypocrites have received their reward already, but we want to receive our God's repayment.

2) Not Praying As the Gentiles Do

The disciples should not pray as the Gentiles do, babbling empty words, supposing that in their multiplicity of words they will be heard. This is because the Father of the disciples knows the things that they need before they ask Him (vv. 7-8). Some have accused us by saying that our pray-reading of the Word is repetitious, but pray-reading is spiritual breathing. Breathing is always repetitious. If we do not repeat our breathing, we will die.

3) Forgiving Men's Offenses

If His disciples forgive men's offenses, their heavenly Father will forgive the disciples also; otherwise, their Father will not forgive their offenses. This annuls their prayer to their heavenly Father (vv. 14-15).

4) Not Fasting like the Sullen-faced Hypocrites

His disciples should not fast like the sullen-faced hypocrites, disfiguring their faces that their fast may appear to men. The disciples should fast by anointing their head and washing their face that their fast may not appear to men but to their Father who is in secret and who sees it and will repay them (vv. 16-18).

2. The Second Time Being
in the Conclusion of His Supreme Teaching
concerning the Kingdom of the Heavens

Now we want to consider the second time the Lord taught the disciples concerning prayer in His supreme teaching on the mount. The second time is in the conclusion of His supreme teaching concerning the kingdom of the heavens, when He made a promise to the seekers of the kingdom of the heavens in Matthew 7:7-8. The Lord said, "Ask [indicating the prayer at a distance] and it shall be given to you; seek [indicating the pursuit of what is prayed for] and you shall find; knock [indicating the reaching of the goal of what is sought] and it shall be opened to you." Such a promise assures the seekers of the kingdom of the heavens that they will be given an open door to enter into all the blessings in the kingdom of the heavens.

When we read the supreme teaching of the Lord on the mount recorded in Matthew 5—7, we may be disappointed and think that we cannot make it because of the supreme, strict requirements. So at the conclusion, there is a prayer which is actually a promise. The Lord promised us that if we ask, we will receive; if we seek, we will find; and if we knock, it will be opened to us. If we ask, seek, and knock, we will enter into all the blessings in the kingdom of the heavens for our supreme and strict kingdom life. This promise affords us the grace that we need to fulfill the supreme and strict requirements. The door will be opened wide for us to enter into all the blessings of the kingdom of the heavens.

THE GOD-MAN LIVING

MESSAGE TWELVE

THE FIRST GOD-MAN'S LIVING
A MAN OF PRAYER

(3)

Scripture Reading: Matt. 9:36—10:4; 11:25-30

OUTLINE

II. The divine facts in the mystical human life of the first God-man in the record of the synoptic Gospels concerning the first God-man as the King-Savior in the kingdom of the heavens, the Slave-Savior in God's gospel service, and the Man-Savior in God's salvation:

C. He taught His disciples to pray concerning the harassed and cast-away sheep of God—Matt. 9:36—10:4:

1. The first God-man as the Shepherd of God's elect, seeing that God's elect were harassed and cast away like sheep not having a shepherd and being moved with compassion, charged His disciples to beseech the Lord of the harvest that He would thrust out workers into His harvest—9:36-38.

2. Then He sent His twelve disciples, who were appointed by Him as the twelve apostles, and gave them authority to cast out unclean spirits and heal all kinds of diseases—10:1-4.

3. In Luke's parallel record of this case, we are told that the Lord Himself "went out to the mountain to pray, and He spent the whole night in prayer to God." The next day He established the twelve apostles to visit and take care of the

people who were troubled by unclean spirits and heal them—Luke 6:12-18.

D. The first God-man, after reproaching the surrounding cities for not being willing to receive His teaching and repent (Matt. 11:20-24), prayed to the Father, and based upon His prayer, He gave a wonderful teaching to His disciples—Matt. 11:25-30:

1. His surpassing prayer to the Father: "I extol You, Father, Lord of heaven and of earth, because You have hidden these things from the wise and intelligent and have revealed them to infants. Yes, Father, for thus it has been well-pleasing in Your sight"—vv. 25-26:

   a. While the first God-man was rebuking the cities, He fellowshipped with the Father, answering the Father by His prayer.

   b. He extolled the Father, acknowledging the Father as Lord of heaven and of earth.

   c. He praised the Father that He has hidden all the things mentioned in verse 27 from the wise and intelligent and has revealed them to infants.

   d. He acknowledged that this has been well-pleasing in the Father's sight and submitted Himself to it.

2. His unveiling teaching to the disciples—vv. 27-30:

   a. All things have been delivered to Him by the Father.

   b. No one fully knows Him except the Father; neither does anyone fully know the Father except Him and him to whom He wills to reveal Him—v. 27.

   c. He calls all who toil and are burdened to come to Him, and He will give them rest—v. 28.

   d. He charges them to take His yoke upon them and learn from Him, for He is meek

and lowly in heart, and they will find rest
for their souls—v. 29.

e. He assures them that His yoke is easy and
His burden is light—v. 30.

In this message we want to cover two examples of prayer uttered by the Lord Jesus, the first God-man. The first prayer is concerning the harassed and cast-away sheep of God in Matthew 9:36—10:4. The second prayer, accompanied by a wonderful teaching, is in Matthew 11:25-30. In this teaching the Lord charged us to take His yoke upon us. We may want to take the Lord's yoke upon us but not know what His yoke is. The yoke of the Lord is the will of the Father. The Lord cared for nothing but the will of His Father (John 4:34; 5:30; 6:38). He submitted Himself fully to the Father's will (Matt. 26:39, 42) according to His economy. The Lord also extolled the Father for His economy.

We must remember that we are still looking at the divine facts in the mystical human life of the first God-man. Every part of the Lord's living on this earth is a divine fact. Whatever God does is a divine fact, and the divine facts were lived in a human life, making that human life mystical. Something divine in humanity is mystical. All the examples of the Lord's prayer are divine facts uttered by Him in His flesh as the man Jesus. A mere human being could not utter such divine sentences. Jesus was a God-man, and all that He said and did are divine facts accomplished in His human life mystically.

C. Teaching His Disciples to Pray concerning the Harassed and Cast-away Sheep of God

This is the third case of prayer in the first God-man's human life. The first case is in Matthew 4 concerning the Lord's fasting. The second is in Matthew 6 and 7 in the Lord's supreme teaching on the mount.

1. Beseeching the Lord of the Harvest to Thrust Out Workers into His Harvest

The first God-man as the Shepherd of God's elect, seeing that God's elect were harassed and cast away as sheep not having a shepherd and being moved with compassion, charged His disciples to beseech the Lord of the harvest that He would thrust out workers into His harvest (Matt. 9:36-38). Prayer is general; beseeching is particular. The Lord of the harvest here is God the Father. We know this because of the parallel record in Luke 6:12-18, which says that the Lord spent the whole night in prayer. If He were the unique Lord of the harvest, He would not have needed to pray to the Father. His prayer indicates that He considered Himself a sent One. He referred to the Father as the One who sent Him (John 8:29) and considered the Father to be the Lord of the harvest.

He charged His disciples to ask the Father not just to send, but to thrust out workers into the harvest. To thrust out is much more forceful than to send. The dear saints who went to Moscow for the Lord's recovery beginning in 1991 were thrust out by the Lord.

2. Sending His Twelve Disciples

Then He sent His twelve disciples, who were appointed by Him as the twelve apostles, and gave them authority to cast out unclean spirits and heal all kinds of diseases (Matt. 10:1-4). Actually, the Lord's sheep were being harassed not merely by men but by the unclean spirits. On the one hand, the demons were harassing them. On the other hand, the Jewish leaders were casting them away. So the Lord sent the twelve apostles to take care of the sheep of God who were under the harassing of evil spirits, demons, and the casting away of the hypocritical Jewish leaders.

3. Luke's Parallel Record

In Luke's parallel record of this case, we are told that the Lord Himself "went out to the mountain to pray, and He spent the whole night in prayer to God." The next day He established the twelve apostles to visit and take care of the people who were troubled by unclean spirits and heal them (Luke 6:12-18). Luke reveals that the Lord's sending was according to the Father's answering of His prayer. He asked the Father who among His followers would be qualified to be apostles. Even Judas, the betrayer, was appointed by the Father's decision for the carrying out of His will.

The Lord went to the mountain completely apart from human society to contact His Father in prayer, and He prayed the whole night. The next day He established the twelve apostles, so His appointment of the twelve apostles should have been according to the Father's answer, decision, and instruction. Matthew did not record this point because Matthew unveils Christ as the King of the kingdom of the heavens. As the King of the kingdom of the heavens, surely He was the Lord of the harvest. But actually, the real Lord of the harvest was the King's Father. Luke's record is on Christ as a proper human, not the King. In Luke this human being went to God the Father to pray.

Now we need to consider what we should learn from the Lord's example. If we saw that a certain brother was harassed, troubled, or sick, what would we do? Perhaps we would not have the heart to care for him. On the other hand, we might care for him and want to do something for him in his need. As a result, we might hurry to see this brother and do things for him. This is our natural doing; it is not divine. Instead, we should learn of the Lord Jesus. We should go to the Lord and pray, "Lord, my brother is very sick. What would You do, Lord? Would You burden me to take care of him? If so, I will bear the burden. If not, I will not do anything by myself as a human being. I want to take care of him with You, to make this care not a human doing but a divine doing." Sometimes when we go to the Lord about a certain needy brother, He may ask us not to contact him at that time, because this brother is in His hand.

All of us who love the church want to help the saints when we see that they are troubled. But if we do this apart from God, it is not divine. To be divine is to do everything with God, by God, in God, and through God. When someone comes to us with a burden or a problem, we should always bring it to the Lord. The Lord may say, "Leave this matter to Me. You stand aside. This is not the thing that you should do." On the other hand, if the Lord burdens us to do something, our doing will be divine.

When the Lord saw God's elect as God's flock harassed and cast away, His heart was moved with compassion. But He did not charge the disciples to directly take care of them. Instead, He told them to pray to the Lord of the harvest and ask Him to thrust out the laborers. The Lord Himself practiced this principle. He saw the need of shepherds for

God's elect, so He spent the whole night in prayer to God. He did not act without prayer. He brought this case to His Father, so He got the Father's decision.

D. His Surpassing Prayer to the Father and His Wonderful Teaching

The first God-man, after reproaching the surrounding cities for not being willing to receive His teaching and repent (Matt. 11:20-24), prayed to the Father, and based upon His prayer, He gave a wonderful teaching to His disciples (vv. 25-30). Most of the time, we cannot pray after reproaching people. If a father cannot pray after reproaching his children, his reproaching was not divine. But if we can still pray after reproaching someone, our reproaching was divine.

1. His Surpassing Prayer

The Lord's surpassing prayer to the Father is as follows: "I extol You, Father, Lord of heaven and of earth, because You have hidden these things from the wise and intelligent and have revealed them to infants. Yes, Father, for thus it has been well-pleasing in Your sight" (vv. 25-26). No one in history has ever prayed such a prayer.

a. Fellowshipping with the Father

While the first God-man was rebuking the cities, He fellowshipped with the Father, answering the Father by His prayer. The Lord's prayer was actually His answering the Father. That indicates that while He was reproaching, He was fellowshipping with the Father. When a father reproaches his children, he should remain in fellowship with the Lord.

b. Extolling the Father

In His prayer the Lord extolled the Father, acknowledging the Father as Lord of heaven and of earth. To extol is to praise with acknowledgment. Mostly we give praise to the Lord without any acknowledgment, but the Lord praised the Father by acknowledging that the Father is the Lord of heaven and earth. We should learn to praise by acknowledging the Father in His economy, His will, and His doing.

When God's people were defeated by His enemy, God was
called "the God of heaven" (Ezra 5:12; Dan. 2:18, 37). But
because Abraham was a man on the earth standing for God,
he called God "the possessor of heaven and earth" (Gen.
14:19, 22). The Lord as the Son of Man called the Father
"Lord of heaven and of earth," indicating that the Lord was
standing on the earth for God's interest. His Father could be
the Lord of the earth through Him and through His disciples.

c. Praising the Father
for Revealing These Things to Infants

The Lord praised the Father that He has hidden all the
things mentioned in Matthew 11:27 from the wise and
intelligent and has revealed them to infants. *The wise and
intelligent* refers to all the peoples in the cities who rejected
the Lord. They were humanly and devilishly wise and
intelligent like today's worldly, intellectual people. The Lord
hides the divine things from them and reveals them to the
disciples, who are the infants.

d. Well-pleasing in the Father's Sight

The Lord acknowledged that this is well-pleasing in the
Father's sight and submitted Himself to it.

2. His Unveiling Teaching to the Disciples

The Lord's prayer is surpassing, and His teaching is
unveiling (vv. 27-30). As the infants, we are unveiled, because
the Lord has taken away all the veils from us.

a. All Things Having Been Delivered to Him by the Father

"All things" here actually refers to all the disciples, the
persons who follow the Lord. In the Gospel of John, the Lord
said repeatedly that all the ones who come to Him and believe
in Him were given to Him by the Father (6:37, 44, 65; 17:6b;
18:9). If the Father had not given us to the Lord Jesus, we
would not be in the church life today. To get us away from
our worldly pursuits was not an easy thing. We are in the
Lord's recovery because the Father has given us to the Lord
Jesus. Our being here is not of ourselves.

b. Knowing the Son and the Father Requiring Revelation

No one fully knows the Son except the Father; neither does anyone fully know the Father except the Son and him to whom the Son wills to reveal Him (Matt. 11:27). Concerning the Son, only the Father has such knowledge, and concerning the Father, only the Son and he to whom the Son reveals Him have such knowledge. Hence, to know the Son requires that the Father reveal Him (16:17), and to know the Father requires that the Son reveal Him (John 17:6, 26). Paul aspired in Philippians 3:10 to know Christ. To know Christ is the preeminent thing. Christ is all-inclusive, all-extensive, and unlimited.

c. Calling All Who Toil and Are Burdened
to Come to Him

The Lord called all who toil and are burdened to come to Him and He would give them rest (Matt. 11:28). The religious Jews were toiling and burdened by working under the law. On this earth who is not toiling or burdened? This world is a toiling world, full of burdens, so the Lord called us to come to Him for rest. Rest means perfect peace and full satisfaction.

d. Charging the Disciples to Take His Yoke upon Them
and Learn from Him

The Lord charged the disciples to take His yoke upon them and learn from Him because He is meek and lowly in heart and they would find rest for their souls (v. 29). To be meek means not to resist opposition, and to be lowly means not to have self-esteem. The rest from the Lord is for our souls; it is an inward rest, not something merely outward in nature. The harassment and the troubles are in our soul. Paul told us to be anxious for nothing and to tell the Lord all our requests. Then the peace of God will guard our hearts and our thoughts in Christ Jesus (Phil. 4:6-7).

e. Assuring Them That His Yoke Is Easy
and His Burden Is Light

The Lord assured the disciples that His yoke is easy and His burden is light (Matt. 11:30). The Greek word for *easy* means "fit for use"; hence, good, kind, mild, gentle, easy, pleasant—in contrast to hard, harsh, sharp, bitter. The yoke of God's economy is like this. Everything in God's economy is not a heavy burden but an enjoyment.

THE GOD-MAN LIVING

THE FIRST GOD-MAN'S LIVING
A MAN OF PRAYER

(4)

A FURTHER WORD
CONCERNING THE FIRST GOD-MAN'S
SURPASSING PRAYER TO HIS FATHER AND
HIS UNVEILING TEACHING TO HIS FOLLOWERS
IN MATTHEW 11:25-30

OUTLINE

I. Regarding God's eternal economy—v. 27:
   A. The Father has delivered all His elect to the Son for the building up of the Son's Body—v. 27a; John 6:37, 44, 65; 17:6b; 18:9.
   B. Only the Father knows the Son as the centrality and universality of His economy—v. 27b; cf. Col. 2:2; Matt. 16:15-17; Gal. 1:15-16; Eph. 3:4; Phil. 3:10.
   C. Only the Son knows the Father as the source and Maker of His economy—v. 27c.
   D. The Son reveals the Father to His believers for the formation of His Body—v. 27d; John 17:6a.
II. Regarding God's pleasant will—vv. 25-26:
   A. The Father has hidden all the things as the contents of His economy from the wise and the intelligent—the worldlings—1 Cor. 1:26.
   B. But He has revealed these things to the infants—the Son's believers—Matt. 19:13-14; 1 Cor. 1:27-28.
   C. This is the Father's pleasant will.
III. Regarding the first God-man as the Head of the Body, the prototype, and the model—vv. 26, 29a:

    A. Being absolutely submissive to God and altogether satisfied with God.

    B. Being meek, not resisting the opponents, and lowly, humbling Himself among men in His heart.

IV. Regarding His believers as the members of His Body, His mass production, and His duplication—vv. 28a, 29b-30:

    A. Answering His call in their heart and coming to Him bodily—v. 28a.

    B. Copying Him in their spirit by taking His yoke—God's will—and toiling for God's economy according to His model—v. 29a; 1 Pet. 2:21.

    C. Sharing in their soul His rest in satisfaction—vv. 28b, 29b, 30.

The Lord's surpassing prayer and His unveiling teaching in Matthew 11:25-30 are regarding four major items: regarding God's eternal economy, regarding God's pleasant will, regarding the first God-man as the Head of the Body, the prototype, and the model, and regarding His believers as the members of His Body, His mass production, and His duplication. The mass production is from the prototype, and the duplication is from the model.

I. REGARDING THE ETERNAL ECONOMY OF GOD

God's eternal economy is seen in Matthew 11:27, where the Lord says, "All things have been delivered to Me by My Father, and no one fully knows the Son except the Father; neither does anyone fully know the Father except the Son and him to whom the Son wills to reveal Him."

A. The Father Having Delivered All His Elect to the Son

The Father has delivered all His elect to the Son for the building up of the Son's Body (v. 27a; John 6:37, 44, 65; 17:6b; 18:9). God the Father has given all His chosen ones to the Son, not for them to go to heaven or merely for their salvation but for the building up of the Body of Christ. The Son needs a Body and the Triune God needs an organism. The Body of Christ is the Triune God's organism for His expression and enlargement. Physically speaking, our body is our enlargement. The Body of Christ as the organism is the enlargement of Christ as the Head. All the elect given to the Son by the Father are the enlargement of Christ and the organism of the Triune God to express Him.

B. Only the Father Knowing the Son

Only the Father knows the Son as the centrality and universality of His economy (Matt. 11:27b; cf. Col. 2:2; Matt. 16:15-17; Gal. 1:15-16; Eph. 3:4; Phil. 3:10). Christ the Son is the mystery of God. God has His person and His purpose. God's person is triune. His Trinity is His person. The content of the New Testament is the Triune God. Every chapter of Ephesians reveals the Triune God (see note 1 of 2 Corinthians

13:14—Recovery Version). Chapter one reveals that God has blessed us in a threefold way. In the Father, He has chosen us; in the Son, He has redeemed us; and in the Spirit, He seals us and is our guarantee. The economy of the Triune God is for Him to dispense Himself into His chosen and redeemed people to make them His expression.

The Triune God's economy was made according to His purpose for His good pleasure, and His good pleasure comes out of His heart's desire. God is a living person, full of feeling. He has His heart's desire. Out of God's heart's desire is God's good pleasure. Out of this pleasure is God's purpose, and out of this purpose is His economy. The entire Bible is the contents of God's economy.

Christ as God came to be a man for God's economy. He is the centrality and universality of God. In January 1934 Brother Watchman Nee gave a conference on Christ being the centrality and universality of God. He is the hub, the rim, and the spokes—the entire content—of God's economy. The first conference I gave in the United States was on the all-inclusive Christ typified by the good land from only three verses—Deuteronomy 8:7-9. To know Christ, as Paul said in Philippians 3:10, is not a small thing, because He is everything. To know any other person is simple because that person is not all-inclusive.

Christ was God becoming a man, and this man who was in the flesh, as the last Adam, became a life-giving Spirit (1 Cor. 15:45b). This life-giving Spirit is compounded with the Divine Trinity, divinity, humanity, Christ's death with its effectiveness, and His resurrection with its power. All these items are compounded into the compound Spirit typified by the anointing ointment in Exodus 30. Also, this compounded, life-giving Spirit became intensified sevenfold (Rev. 1:4; 4:5; 5:6). The New Testament reveals Christ in the flesh in the Gospels, Christ as the life-giving Spirit in the Epistles, and Christ as the sevenfold intensified life-giving Spirit in Revelation. No one can know Christ the Son in an exhaustive way except the Father. The Son is the Father's word, explanation, definition, and expression.

C. Only the Son Knowing the Father

Only the Son knows the Father as the source and Maker of His economy (Matt. 11:27c). No one fully knows the Father except the Son and those believers to whom the Son wills to reveal the Father. The four Gospels show us God the Father. No other book reveals the Father as much as the Gospel of John does. We have seen that the Lord Jesus extolled the Father as the Lord of heaven and earth (v. 25). He praised the Father with acknowledgment.

D. The Son Revealing the Father to His Believers

The Son reveals the Father to His believers for the formation of His Body (v. 27d; John 17:6a). God's economy is for the expression of the Father through the Son with His organism, the Body of Christ. The New Testament teaches that the Father as the source has a desire to have an organism through the Son, and the Son came to call God's elect to come to Him so that He can regenerate, sanctify, and transform them, making them His Body to be the organism of the Triune God.

The New Testament teaches us, the members of the Body of Christ, to do everything with God, in God, by God, and through God. It does not teach us to love people in an ethical way with our natural love. We have to love others by and with God, in a divine and mystical way. His love is divine, but the outward lover is a mystical human. The Bible teaches us to live as divine and mystical persons.

II. REGARDING GOD'S PLEASANT WILL

A. The Father Hiding the Contents of His Economy from the Wise and Intelligent

The Father has hidden all the things as the contents of His economy from the wise and the intelligent—the worldlings. In 1 Corinthians 1:26 Paul said, "For consider your calling, brothers, that there are not many wise according to flesh, not many powerful, not many wellborn." The universities are full of wise and intelligent men who are blind concerning God's economy.

B. Revealing These Things to the Infants

The Father has revealed these things to the infants—the Son's believers (Matt. 19:13-14; 1 Cor. 1:27-28). In Matthew 19, when people brought the infants to the Lord Jesus, the disciples rebuked them. But the Lord said, "Allow the little children and do not prevent them from coming to Me, for of such is the kingdom of the heavens" (v. 14). If we are wise and intelligent and not as children, there is no hope for us to enter into the kingdom of the heavens.

C. The Father's Pleasant Will

It is the Father's pleasant will to hide the contents of His economy from the wise and intelligent, the worldlings, and reveal them to infants, the Son's believers.

III. REGARDING THE FIRST GOD-MAN AS THE HEAD OF THE BODY, THE PROTOTYPE, AND THE MODEL

The first God-man is the Head of the Body, the prototype, and the model (Matt. 11:29a). He came as one grain of wheat to produce many grains (John 12:24). The one grain was the prototype, and the many grains are the mass production. The mass production is the duplication of the model. Peter told us that Christ is a model to the believers (1 Pet. 2:21). The Greek word for *model* is literally a writing copy, an underwriting used by students to trace letters and thereby learn to draw them. We become the reproduction of Christ as the original writing copy. Christ is the prototype to produce a mass production and the model to produce the many duplications.

A. Being Absolutely Submissive to God and Altogether Satisfied with God

Christ was the first God-man, and we are the many God-men. We have to learn of Him in His absolute submission to God and His uttermost satisfaction with God. Christ was so submissive to and satisfied with the Father and His will.

B. Being Meek, Not Resisting the Opponents, and Lowly, Humbling Himself among Men in His Heart

The Lord was meek, meaning that He did not resist His opponents. He was also lowly, meaning that He humbled Himself among men in His heart.

IV. REGARDING HIS BELIEVERS AS THE MEMBERS OF HIS BODY, HIS MASS PRODUCTION, AND HIS DUPLICATION

A. Answering His Call in Their Heart

The Lord's believers answer His call in their heart and come to Him bodily (Matt. 11:28a). To come to Him bodily means that our entire being has to come to Him. This is why Paul charges us in Romans 12:1 to present our bodies to the Lord as a living sacrifice. We have to present our bodies in a practical way by being in the meetings of the church. Since I was saved by the Lord in 1925, I have come to Him with my entire being.

B. Copying Him in Their Spirit

The believers copy the Lord in their spirit by taking His yoke—God's will—and toiling for God's economy according to His model (Matt. 11:29a; 1 Pet. 2:21). The Lord told us to learn from Him. To learn from Him is to copy Him, not to imitate Him outwardly. In this way we become His duplication and mass production. The first requirement in learning from Him is to take His yoke, which is God's will. God's will has to yoke us, and we have to put our neck into this yoke. Seventy years ago as a young man, I took the yoke of Jesus. That yoke has protected me for the past seventy years.

We also need to be those who toil for God's economy. All the worldly people are toiling and are burdened in many things. They are very busy. The Lord is calling those who are toiling, who are burdened, and who have no rest or satisfaction, to come to Him so that He can give them the real rest with satisfaction. The rest without satisfaction is not the real rest. We take His yoke and toil for God's economy according to His model, following Him in His footsteps.

C. Sharing in Their Soul His Rest in Satisfaction

The hardest thing is to rest in our soul. People lose sleep because their soul is bothered. The rest that we find by taking the Lord's yoke and learning from Him is for our soul. We share in our soul His rest in satisfaction (Matt. 11:28b, 29b, 30).

THE GOD-MAN LIVING

MESSAGE FOURTEEN

THE FIRST GOD-MAN'S LIVING
A MAN OF PRAYER

(5)

Scripture Reading: Matt. 14:19, 23

OUTLINE

II. The divine facts in the mystical human life of the first God-man in the record of the synoptic Gospels concerning the first God-man as the King-Savior in the kingdom of the heavens, the Slave-Savior in God's gospel service, and the Man-Savior in God's salvation:
  E. In the performing of the miracle of feeding five thousand people with five loaves and two fish, He trained His disciples to learn from Him (Matt. 11:29) that:
    1. Before performing the miracle, He took the five loaves and two fish, looked up to heaven (indicating that He looked up to His Father in heaven), and blessed them (Matt. 14:19), indicating that:
      a. As the Son on earth sent by the Father in heaven, He was one with the Father, trusting in the Father—John 10:30.
      b. He did not do anything from Himself—John 5:19.
      c. He did not seek His own will but the will of Him who sent Him—John 5:30b.
      d. He did not seek His own glory but the glory of the Father who sent Him—John 7:18.
    2. After performing the miracle, He went up to

the mountain privately to pray (Matt. 14:23; cf.
Luke 6:12), indicating that:

a. He did not remain in the issue of the miracle
   with the crowds but went away from them
   privately to be with the Father on the
   mountain in prayer.

b. He might ask the Father to bless all those
   who had participated in the enjoyment of
   the issue of the miracle:

   1) That they would not be satisfied with the
      food which perishes;

   2) But that they should seek for the food
      which abides unto eternal life;

   3) And recognize that He was not only the
      Son of Man but also the Son of God:

      a) Who was sent and sealed by the
         Father,

      b) And who could give them the eternal
         life—John 6:27.

c. He might receive of the Father some instruction concerning how to take care of the
   five thousand people fed by His miracle.

In this message we want to continue our fellowship concerning the Lord's pattern as a man of prayer in the record of Matthew.

E. Training His Disciples to Learn from Him in the Miracle of Feeding Five Thousand People

1. Taking the Five Loaves and Two Fish, Looking Up to Heaven, and Blessing Them

In the performing of the miracle of feeding five thousand people with five loaves and two fish, He trained His disciples to learn from Him. In Matthew 11:29 the Lord told the disciples that they needed to learn from Him, indicating that He was their pattern.

Matthew 14:19 says that He took the five loaves and two fish and when He was going to bless them, He looked up to heaven. In other words, He blessed the food by looking up to heaven. *Looking up to heaven* indicates that He was looking up to His Father in heaven. This indicates that He realized the source of the blessing was not Him. He was the sent One. The sent One should not be the source of blessing. The sending One, the Father, should be the source of blessing.

Here is a great lesson for us to learn. Most readers of the Bible would pay attention to the miracle of creating something from nothing performed by the Lord Jesus in Matthew 14. But we need to see the pattern which the Lord set up for us here. We need to remember that He looked up to the Father in heaven and blessed the five loaves and two fish in front of His disciples. After His blessing in this way, He told the disciples what to do. No doubt, what He did was a pattern for the disciples to learn from Him. According to this pattern, we have to realize that we are not the Sender, but the ones sent by the Sender. Regardless of how much we can do, we should realize that we still need the blessing from the source, from our Sender, that we can pass on to the benefited ones. This is a big lesson which I want to stress.

A co-worker who is invited to speak somewhere may think that since he has been speaking for the Lord for many years, he knows how to speak. All of us need to drop this kind of attitude and realize that we are not the source. No blessing is of us. Regardless of how much we can do or how much we know what to do, we must realize that we need the Sender's blessing upon our doing by trusting in Him, not in ourselves. Even when we take our meals, we should learn of the Lord to look up to the Father as the source. When we bless our food, we should bless it by looking up to the source of blessing.

a. Being One with the Father

His looking up to the Father in heaven indicated that as the Son on earth sent by the Father in heaven, He was one with the Father, trusting in the Father (John 10:30). This is a very important principle. Whenever I speak for the Lord, I must have the sensation that I am one with the Lord, trusting in Him. What I know and what I can do mean nothing. Being one with the Lord and trusting in Him mean everything in our ministry. We should never go to minister the word by remaining in ourselves and by trusting in what we can do. If we trust in what we can do, we are finished. The blessing comes only by our being one with the Lord and trusting in Him.

b. Not Doing Anything from Himself

The Lord did not do anything from Himself (John 5:19). This was also a pattern to the disciples. He was the One through whom the entire universe was created, but He would not do anything from Himself. This is the denying of our self, which He taught so much. He said that anyone who follows Him must take up his cross and deny himself (Matt. 16:24). He lived a life of denying Himself.

The learned professors in the universities do many things in order to attract people's attention, displaying what they know and can do. But we are not today's professors; we are today's God-men, the duplication of Jesus. We should deny ourselves and not have the intention of doing anything from ourselves but have the intention of doing everything from Him. This is to practice the teaching of denying the self by doing things with the Lord.

c. Not Seeking His Own Will

The Lord did not seek His own will but the will of Him who sent Him (John 5:30b). First, He denied Himself; second, He rejected His idea, His intention, and His purpose. He would only seek the will of the One who sent Him. All of us should be on the alert for this one thing—when we are sent to do some work, we should not take that chance to seek our own goal. When we go to perform God's work, do we go by seeking our purpose or God's purpose? Brother Watchman Nee was always concerned that when he sent a brother out for the Lord's work, that brother would take the chance to perform his own purpose.

One day I was preparing to go from Shanghai to Hangchow. Then Brother Nee asked me, "Witness, for what purpose are you going to Hangchow?" I responded that I was going to visit the brothers there. He said that this was a wrong answer. Instead, I should say that I am going to perform the Lord's purpose. If you merely go to visit the brothers, you can do many things for yourself. You may take your visit to them as a chance for you to accomplish your purpose instead of seeking the Lord's will. It is not easy to have a pure heart, without having our purpose, our goal, and our idea. We should just go seeking the idea, purpose, goal, and intention of the sending Lord. This requires much learning on our part.

At times certain brothers may ask me how I feel about their accepting the invitation to a certain place. My basic consideration is, "Are you going just to fulfill the Lord's purpose, the Lord's aim, the Lord's goal, the Lord's idea, the Lord's intention, that is, the Lord's will, or would you take the chance to accomplish your intention, your will?" To seek our intention is absolutely impure. We need to be purified by the cross. We should pray, "Lord, save me from going out to accomplish something according to my intention and idea." The Lord Jesus never sought His own idea, His own purpose, His own concept, or His own intention. He purely sought only the Father's will.

d. Not Seeking His Own Glory

The first God-man did not seek His own glory but the glory of the Father who sent Him (John 7:18). I was with Brother Nee for about twenty years. What bothered him the most about the co-workers was that it was hard to see one who was not ambitious. To be ambitious is to seek your own glory. In the service we render to the Lord in the church life, there is always our ambition. A brother may have the ambition to be an elder. In order to become an elder, he feels that he must first become a deacon. To him being a deacon is a step toward being uplifted to the eldership. We should not think that we are absolutely not ambitious in this way. We are all fallen descendants of Adam and sick of the same disease, the same sin. The rebellion that occurred among us seven years ago was altogether due to ambition. Through the years I have seen a number of co-workers among us spoiled by ambition. By the Lord's mercy, I have learned the secret of dealing with my self and my intention, and this has helped me to deal with my self-glorification.

In John 7:18 the Lord told the Pharisees, "He who speaks from himself seeks his own glory; but He who seeks the glory of Him who sent Him, this One is true, and unrighteousness is not in Him." The Pharisees were seeking their own glory. According to the context of this verse, the Lord indicated to them that if they were not seeking their own glory, they would know that He was sent by His Father.

We need to see that our self, our purpose, and our ambition are three big destroying "worms" in our work. If we are going to be used for the Lord always in His recovery, our self has to be denied, our purpose has to be rejected, and our ambition must be given up. We should not have our own purpose; instead, we should have only the Lord's will. We all have to learn of these three things: no self, no purpose, and no ambition. We should only know to labor, to work for Him, by denying our self, rejecting our purpose, and giving up our ambition. Self, purpose, and ambition are like three snakes or scorpions in us. We must learn to hate them.

2. *Going Up to the Mountain Privately to Pray*

After performing the miracle, the Lord went up to the mountain privately to pray (Matt. 14:23; cf. Luke 6:12).

a. *Not Remaining in the Issue of the Miracle with the Crowds*

The Lord did not remain in the issue of the miracle with the crowds but went away from them privately to be with the Father on the mountain in prayer. If we go to a certain place and have a great success, would we leave right away or would we remain in this big success to enjoy it? We need to see and follow the pattern of the Lord Jesus. He did not remain in the issue of the great miracle which He performed. Instead, He went up to the mountain privately to pray. The word *privately* is very meaningful. This means He did not let the people know He was going to pray. Otherwise, they would have followed Him. He went away from them privately to be with the Father in prayer. I like these three phrases: *to be with the Father, on the mountain,* and *in prayer.* We should learn from the Lord's pattern here by exercising to be with Him on the mountain in prayer. His looking up to heaven means that He had no trust in Himself. His going up to the mountain means that He wanted to be with the Father in prayer.

To pray with others is good, but often we need to pray by ourselves. When we pray with others, we cannot enjoy the Lord as deeply as when we pray to the Lord privately. Even the Lord Jesus told us that when we pray we should shut our door privately and pray secretly to the Father who sees in secret (Matt. 6:6). Then we have the sensation of how intimate He is to us and how close we are to Him. We have to learn to leave the crowds, our family, our friends, and the saints in the church to go to a higher level on a "high mountain." We have to go higher, far away from the earthly things on a lower level. We need to get to a higher level, separated from the crowd, to be with the Father privately and secretly to have intimate fellowship with Him. This is the significance of being *on the mountain in prayer.*

b. Asking the Father to Bless All Those Who Participated
in the Enjoyment of the Issue of the Miracle

We need to consider why the Lord Jesus went to the
mountain right after this miracle. John 6:27 gives us the
reason. This verse says that after performing the miracle,
the Lord said: "Work not for the food which perishes, but for
the food which abides unto eternal life, which the Son of Man
will give you; for Him has the Father, even God, sealed." The
Lord told the ones whom He fed not to seek the food that
perishes, but to seek the food that abides unto eternal life. I
believe the Lord Jesus went to the mountain to pray in this
way: "Father, I pray to You under Your blessing. Through
Your blessing You fed the five thousand, but Father, they are
just seeking for the food that perishes. I do look unto You
that You would bless them that they would seek the food that
abides unto eternal life. Father, You know that I am Your
sent One. Only I can give them the food that abides unto
eternal life, but they do not know Me in this way. They know
only that I can perform a miracle to feed them with physical
food. But they do not know that it is only I who can give
them food that is of the eternal life." I believe that the Lord
prayed to bless them further in this way.

His going up to the mountain privately to pray indicated
His asking the Father to bless all those who had participated
in the enjoyment of the issue of the miracle that they would
not be satisfied with the food which perishes, but that they
should seek for the food which abides unto eternal life and
recognize that He was not only the Son of Man but also the
Son of God who was sent and sealed by the Father and who
could give them eternal life. When the five thousand were
being fed by Him, they recognized that He was the capable
Son of Man, but they did not realize that He was actually
the Son of God who was not only sent but also sealed by the
Father. He was the One who could give them the very bread
that is related to the eternal life. For this reason, He had
another teaching in John 6. In John 6 the Lord revealed that
He is the bread out of heaven, the bread of life. Eventually,
He told us that this bread is just His word. "The words which

I have spoken to you are spirit and are life" (v. 63). John 3:34 says that He is the One who speaks the word and gives the Spirit not by measure. To know Him in this way requires a revelation, so He prayed for them privately on the mountain.

c. Receiving Some Instruction from the Father

His going up to the mountain privately to pray also indicated that He wanted to receive of the Father some instruction concerning how to take care of the five thousand people fed by His miracle.

In this crystallization-study of Matthew 14, we can see how much we need revelation from the Lord to see the intrinsic significance of His word. To see the miracle of feeding five thousand with five loaves and two fish is easy, but to know the deeper lessons which we have to learn from the Performer of this big miracle requires revelation. These lessons are intrinsic, deeper, and of life. To know the great miracle the Lord performed does not give us any life. We can only admire the Lord's outward doing. But to see all the detailed points concerning the lessons of life to learn from the Lord in His way of performing the miracle imparts life to us. We need to learn these living lessons from the Lord so that we can enter into the God-man living.

THE GOD-MAN LIVING

THE FIRST GOD-MAN'S LIVING
A MAN OF PRAYER

(6)

Scripture Reading: Matt. 15:36-39; 17:19-21; 18:15-22; 19:13-15

OUTLINE

II. The divine facts in the mystical human life of the first God-man in the record of the synoptic Gospels concerning the first God-man as the King-Savior in the kingdom of the heavens, the Slave-Savior in God's gospel service, and the Man-Savior in God's salvation:

F. In the performing of the miracle of feeding four thousand people with seven loaves and a few small fish (Matt. 15:36-39), He trained His disciples again to learn from Him that:

1. Before performing the miracle, He gave thanks (Matt. 15:36), indicating that:

   a. He honored His Father as the source of the supply of the people's necessities, standing on the position of One sent by His Father.

   b. He trained His disciples to give thanks to God the Father for their necessities and in everything (1 Thes. 5:18; Eph. 5:20).

2. After performing the miracle, He left the crowd and went to the borders of Magadan (Matt. 15:39), indicating that He would not remain in the issue of the miracle with the crowd for the enjoyment of their appreciation.

G. In answering His disciples' question concerning why they were not able to cast out a demon (17:19-21), He trained them that:

       1. They should pray with faith—v. 20.

       2. They should also pray with fasting—v. 21.

H. In dealing with one who is disobedient to the church (18:15-22), He trained His disciples:

       1. To bind the disobedient one with their heavenly authority by two or three of them meeting together to pray for the disobedient one in harmony—vv. 18-20.

       2. To forgive the offending one (this might indicate the disobedient one) up to seventy times seven times—vv. 21-22.

I. When people brought their children to Him that He might lay His hands on them and pray but His disciples rebuked them (19:13-15), He trained them:

       1. By correcting them not to prevent the little children but to allow them to come to Him, indicating that the kingdom of the heavens is of such—v. 14.

       2. By laying His hands on the little children—v. 15.

We have seen from Matthew 11 that the Lord Jesus told us we have to learn from Him (v. 29). He is our prototype and also our model. We have to be His reproduction and His copy. When the Lord fed the five thousand with five loaves and two fish, as recorded in Matthew 14, He did that for the disciples to learn from Him, not just for them to see a big miracle. The Lord cares for the lessons of life.

F. In the Performing of the Miracle of Feeding Four Thousand People

1. Giving Thanks before Performing the Miracle

In the performing of the miracle of feeding four thousand people with seven loaves and a few small fish (Matt. 15:36-39), He trained His disciples again to learn from Him. This was the second time that He fed a great multitude. The first time, when He fed the five thousand, He blessed the loaves and the fish, looking up to heaven. His blessing was under the blessing from the Father who is in heaven. Before feeding the four thousand, He gave thanks to God (v. 36). I believe the Lord did this purposely for the training of the disciples.

a. Honoring His Father as the Source

His giving thanks indicated that He honored His Father as the source of the supply of the people's necessities, standing on the position of One sent by the Father. This indicated to His disciples that His Father, not He, was the source of all the necessities of the people. Otherwise, people would give the glory to Him, thinking that He was the source. As the sent One, the Lord Jesus gave thanks to the Sender. He stood on the position of One sent by His Father.

Satan is the opposite of the Lord Jesus. The Lord Jesus stood on His position as a sent One, a subordinate, not the source. But Satan rebelled against the source to exalt himself. That became a rebellion which caused the entire universe to become chaos. Not only are humans fighting on this earth, but also, according to Daniel, the angels are fighting (10:13, 20). The Bible shows us clearly that there are two kinds of angels: the good angels standing with God and the bad ones following Satan. In Revelation 12 Satan is likened to a great red dragon whose tail drags away the third part of the stars of heaven (vv. 3-4). The stars of heaven here signify the angels (Job 38:7; Isa. 14:12). The third part of the stars of heaven are the fallen angels who followed Satan in his rebellion against God. There is war taking place both on the earth and in the heavens. Today the earth is full of rebellion and fighting. The United Nations attempts to keep the peace but there is no way for them to do it. Even in the church, disorder appears, so according to the New Testament teaching the Lord Jesus set up a model to keep a good order. He always stood on the position of a sent One from the Father.

When He performed miracles, He was also in the status of a man. During the three and a half years of His earthly ministry, He acted as a man submissive to God. This put Satan to shame. This is why the Lord said that in Him Satan had nothing (John 14:30b). Satan has nothing in Him because His submission to the Father cuts off Satan. Today in the Lord's recovery, we must learn how to keep a proper order of submission in the Body. Brother Watchman Nee stressed this greatly. The Lord did not teach this much, but He behaved in this way to train His disciples. That was why He told His disciples to take His yoke and learn from Him. Today we have to follow the Lord's pattern. We have to take Him as the model to copy, honoring the Father as the source of the supply of the people's necessities, standing on the position of the One sent by His Father.

b. Training His Disciples to Give Thanks to God the Father

He also trained His disciples to give thanks to God the Father for their necessities and in everything. In both 1 Thessalonians 5:18 and Ephesians 5:20 Paul told us to give thanks to God in everything. This is very important. We do not want to make anything a mere formality. But still in doing everything, even in common things, we have to say, "Lord, I thank You for this. Everything You have created has been prepared to meet my need by Your mercy and by Your divine provision." We need to thank the Lord for all of His physical and spiritual blessings.

2. *After Performing the Miracle, Leaving the Crowd and Going to the Borders of Magadan*

After He fed the five thousand, He left the crowd to go to the high mountain privately to pray (Matt. 14:23). After feeding the four thousand, He also left the crowd and went to the borders of Magadan (15:39), indicating that He would not remain in the issue of the miracle with the crowd for the enjoyment of their appreciation. This is a pattern to us. Whenever we speak and have a good meeting, we want to stay with the crowd to enjoy people's appreciation. That is fleshly. In the first feeding, the Lord left and went to the mountain privately. The next time He left the appreciating crowd and went to the locality of Magadan.

G. Answering His Disciples' Question concerning Why They Were Not Able to Cast Out a Demon

1. Praying with Faith

The disciples could not succeed in attempting to cast out a demon, so they asked the Lord why this was so. In His answer to their question, He trained them that they should pray with faith (17:19-20). In the early years in China among us, there were a number of cases of casting out demons, but not in recent years. If we try to cast out demons, they will condemn us. When they condemn us, we can lose our assurance, causing us to pray without faith. This is why we have to declare, "Satan, you are defeated. You are the defeated enemy, and the Lord Jesus crossed you out on the cross. We have the blood of the Lamb that covers us and that overcomes your accusation." This is the word of our testimony which defeats the devil (see Rev. 12:11 and note 3). This gives us the assurance to pray with faith.

2. Praying with Fasting

The Lord also said that we need to pray with fasting (Matt. 17:21). Sometimes the demons are very persistent to struggle and not go away. This is why we need to pray with faith and also with fasting. These two things—faith and fasting—put down our natural being, our flesh. If we are in the flesh, we

can neither have faith nor fast in a genuine way. To pray
with faith is to contact God and to be saturated with God,
resulting in having faith in God for the exaltation of God,
and to fast is to deal with the self, putting down ourselves.

H. In Dealing with One
Who Is Disobedient to the Church

1. To Bind the Disobedient One
with Their Heavenly Authority

In dealing with one who is disobedient to the church, the
Lord trained His disciples to bind the disobedient one with
their heavenly authority by two or three of them meeting
together to pray for the disobedient one in harmony (18:18-20).
Matthew 18:15-22 describes the case of a brother who is
disobedient first to someone who wants to shepherd him.
Because he will not listen, this shepherding one takes one or
two more with him. If he still rebels, they tell it to the church.
If he will not hear the church, he will lose the fellowship of
the church and will be like the Gentile and the tax collector,
those who are outside the fellowship of the church.

The Lord Jesus told the disciples to bind such rebellious
ones with the authority from the heavens. What we bind will
be bound in heaven. The elders especially have to learn how
to bind the rebellious ones. We should not bind someone
outwardly in a fleshly way. We have to bind with the authority
of the heavens by two or three coming together in the
principle of the Body, not by ourselves. Two or three represent
the cooperation of the Body.

These two or three do not come together to discuss things
but to pray in harmony. There is the need of the harmony
among men to have the heavenly authority. To pray in
harmony is as musical sounds are in harmony. Whatever we
say in binding a rebellious one must be like music to God
and also to the enemy Satan for him to be defeated. If we
are inwardly opinionated and dissenting, the devil knows our
hearts. It is very difficult for husbands and wives to be in
harmony. Even in the church life, it can be the same among
the saints. As long as the elders are not in harmony, the

eldership is lost. They will not be able to exercise the Lord's authority.

Whoever is not in harmony to the extent that he rebels in the church life will suffer loss. The Lord Jesus set up an example which is a real shame to Satan, who is the great rebel. In the universe there is one person by the name of Jesus Christ who submitted Himself absolutely and continuously to His Father, standing in His own position to keep the harmony among the Trinity.

2. To Forgive the Offending One

Matthew 18:21 and 22 say, "Then Peter came and said to Him, Lord, how often shall my brother sin against me and I forgive him? Up to seven times? Jesus said to him, I do not say to you, Up to seven times, but, Up to seventy times seven." According to the context of these verses, the offending one might be the disobedient one in the previous section. It might be that Peter was offended at a disobedient brother. Because he was strong and outspoken, Peter asked the Lord how many times he should forgive his brother. The Lord said that if we are going to forgive a disobedient brother, we have to forgive him seventy times seven, that is, 490 times. To bind is easy; to forgive is hard. The wives and the husbands should not bind each other, but forgive each other. The ones who live the kingdom life in the heavens do not have the feeling of being offended. The more we live in the kingdom, the less we feel that some have offended us, even though they may have done many wrong things to us.

I. People Bringing Their Children to the Lord

People brought their children to the Lord that He might lay His hands on them and pray, but His disciples rebuked them (Matt. 19:13-15).

1. Correcting the Disciples

The Lord trained the disciples by correcting them not to prevent the little children but to allow them to come to Him, indicating that the kingdom of the heavens is of such (v. 14). All the kingdom people should be like children. For the disciples to rebuke the children coming to the Lord indicates that they felt that they were mature and special. We should never be proud in this way. We should never reject the weaker ones, the fallen ones, the mistaken and backsliding ones, or the ones whom we feel are not growing. In the service of the Lord, we have to take care of such ones. Paul in Galatians 6 charged us to recover in a spirit of meekness the ones overtaken by sin (v. 1).

2. Laying His Hands on the Little Children

The Lord also trained the disciples by laying His hands on the little children (Matt. 19:15). The Lord's blessing goes with His hand. His laying His hands on the little ones indicates that He would never reject any weaker ones, mistaken ones, or defeated ones, who are like children. The Lord would not forget them; He would still give them the blessing. All these points are very instructive and show us how we should deal with people and be among them for the Lord's interests.

THE GOD-MAN LIVING

MESSAGE SIXTEEN

THE FIRST GOD-MAN'S LIVING
A MAN OF PRAYER

(7)

Scripture Reading: Matt. 21:18-22; Mark 11:20-24; Matt. 24:15-22; 26:20-30, 36-46

OUTLINE

II. The divine facts in the mystical human life of the first God-man in the record of the synoptic Gospels concerning the first God-man as the King-Savior in the kingdom of the heavens, the Slave-Savior in God's gospel service, and the Man-Savior in God's salvation:

J. In cursing the fig tree so that it instantly dried up, the first God-man taught His disciples how to pray by faith—Matt. 21:18-22; Mark 11:20-24:

1. The first God-man's teaching here was according to God's will to be accomplished for the fulfillment of His economy:

   a. The fig tree is a symbol of the nation of Israel (Jer. 24:2, 5, 8).

   b. The nation of Israel lost her capacity in fulfilling God's economy because of her rottenness.

   c. Because their condition of not bearing fruit but having only leaves still remained after the first God-man's ministry among them, God intended to give them up—Matt. 21:33-43.

   d. At this juncture, the first God-man cursed her to dry up, according to God's will in fulfilling His economy—Matt. 21:19.

2. Based upon this background, the first God-man taught His disciples to pray for executing God's will according to His economy by faith—Matt. 21:21-22.

3. Thus, the praying one could have faith in God without doubting, but believing that he had received what he asked for, and he would have it—Mark 11:24.

K. In prophesying that the returned Israel in the future will suffer the great tribulation, the first God-man taught them here how to flee by prayer— Matt. 24:15-22:

1. They should ask God that their flight may not be in winter nor on a Sabbath—v. 20.

2. They should believe that God is the One who controls the weather and the surrounding environment.

L. In His prayer in Gethsemane before He was arrested, judged, and sentenced to be crucified, He prayed and taught His disciples to learn from Him how to pray—Matt. 26:20-30, 36-46:

1. After the Feast of the Passover He taught His disciples how to remember Him by breaking the bread and drinking the cup—vv. 20, 26-29.

2. He was burdened to go to Gethsemane, a quiet place, deep in the night, with His disciples, to pray—vv. 30, 36.

3. He took Peter, John, and James aside and began to be sorrowful and deeply distressed, saying to them, "My soul is exceedingly sorrowful, even to death," and asking them to remain there and watch with Him—vv. 37-38:

   a. He went forward a little, fell on His face, and prayed, saying, "My Father, if it is possible, let this cup pass from Me; yet not as I will, but as You will"—v. 39.

   b. He went away a second time and prayed, saying, "My Father, if this cannot pass away unless I drink it, Your will be done"—v. 42.

    c. He left them and went away again and prayed a third time, saying the same word again—v. 44.

4. The first God-man's prayer here, like all His prayers in the synoptic Gospels, was prayed by Him in His humanity; this prayer here, made by Him when He was exceedingly sorrowful and deeply distressed, corresponds with the one in Paul's writing in Hebrews 5:7 in which He offered up both petitions and supplications with strong crying and tears, asking God to save Him out of death.

5. This prayer was after Christ's prayer in John 17 as the conclusion of His divine teaching in John 14—16 concerning the union, mingling, and incorporation of the processed and consummated Triune God with His chosen and redeemed people, which was prayed in Christ's divinity. (We will cover this prayer in the summer training on the Crystallization-study of the Gospel of John.)

We have been fellowshipping concerning the prayers of the first God-man made by Him in His humanity as the King-Savior in the kingdom of the heavens. All the prayers offered by the Lord in Matthew, Mark, and Luke—the synoptic Gospels—were made by Christ in His humanity. These prayers are in a different category from His prayer in John 17. This prayer was offered by the Lord after His discourse in John 14 through 16 concerning the union, mingling, and incorporation of the processed and consummated Triune God with His chosen and redeemed people. It was offered by Christ to God not in His humanity but in His divinity.

In this message we want to see three more cases of Christ's prayer in the Gospel of Matthew. We need to see that these prayers are related to God's will for the accomplishment of God's economy.

J. In Cursing the Fig Tree, Teaching His Disciples How to Pray by Faith

In cursing the fig tree so that it instantly dried up, the first God-man taught His disciples how to pray by faith (Matt. 21:18-22; Mark 11:20-24).

1. His Teaching Being according to God's Will

The first God-man's teaching here was according to God's will to be accomplished for the fulfillment of His economy. Not many see that the Lord's teaching on prayer is related to God's economy, which is to be accomplished by His faithful people doing His will. The One who taught the disciples to pray by faith was the God-man, Christ. He is the only One who is absolutely right before God. To pray such a prayer we must be right persons doing God's will. This is God's will not in small matters, such as where we should move, but His great will for the accomplishment of God's economy. Many Christians today use the term *the will of God* in a very shallow and light way. We should be those who are carrying out God's will to accomplish God's economy. God's economy is to produce an organism for His good pleasure. Israel disappointed God in this matter, so God came to the church, hoping that the church would be His organism. Eventually, the church, generally speaking, has also failed God. What is the real will of God that we have to carry out? It is to take care of the producing and building up of God's organism, which is the Body of Christ that will consummate the New Jerusalem.

a. The Symbol of the Fig Tree

The fig tree is a symbol of the nation of Israel (Jer. 24:2, 5, 8).

b. Israel Losing Her Capacity in Fulfilling God's Economy

The nation of Israel lost her capacity in fulfilling God's economy because of her rottenness. In Revelation 2, the Lord's first epistle to the first church, at Ephesus, says that because the church there lost her capacity to shine forth the testimony of Jesus, the Lord would remove her lampstand (v. 5). The same thing occurred to Israel in the ancient time. Actually, Israel was a lampstand, established by God to stand on the whole earth to shine forth God's testimony (Zech. 4:2), but she lost this capacity because of her rottenness.

c. The Condition of Not Bearing Fruit

Because the people of Israel's condition of not bearing fruit but having only leaves still remained after the first God-man's ministry among them, God intended to give them up (Matt. 21:33-43). The Lord ministered among them for three and a half years. No doubt, He was the top Minister and His ministry was the top ministry, but it had no effect on this nation chosen by God, so God intended to give them up. The Lord used a parable in Matthew 21:33-43 to tell them that the kingdom of God would be taken from them and given to a nation producing its fruit. This nation is the church.

d. Cursing the Fig Tree So That It Dried Up, according to God's Will in Fulfilling His Economy

The Lord Jesus, who is right in the eyes of God, knows God's heart, so His cursing the fig tree was according to His knowledge of God's will in the fulfillment of God's economy to give up the rotten Israel (Matt. 21:19).

2. *Teaching His Disciples to Pray*

Based upon this background, the first God-man taught His disciples to pray for executing God's will according to His economy by faith (Matt. 21:21-22).

3. *Having Faith in God without Doubting*

Thus, the praying one could have faith in God without doubting, but believing that he had received what he asked for, and he would have it (Mark 11:24). The praying one is now one with God, in union with God. He is mingled with God, so God becomes his faith. This is what it means to have faith in God, according to the Lord's word in Mark 11:22. The praying one is absolutely one with God, and God becomes his faith.

In Mark 11:24 the Lord said, "All things that you pray and ask, believe that you have received them, and you will have them." I would like to present two testimonies concerning the experience of this verse. The first one is concerning the Lord's move to Russia. Soon after the United States defeated Iraq in 1991, one day a thought came to me: "Why don't you go to Russia? Now is the time." When I fellowshipped with the leading co-workers about this, they all agreed with me, so we announced to the saints that we would follow the Lord's leading to go to Russia. Right away there was a response from the Body for this move of the Lord. This is a testimony that I had the full faith that we received a success. By the time we decided to go to Russia, a number of the saints had been trained and prepared by finishing two terms of the full-time training in Anaheim. They responded that they would go, and in November 1991 over thirty went to Russia. Right away the financial support came from the churches. In Russia today there are two big churches in Moscow and St. Petersburg. Recently, thirty-five more churches have been established. Also, there are numerous locations with groups of seeking Christians who have left the denominations and are waiting for us to visit them to help establish them as local churches. The brothers have estimated that by the end of this year, there will be fifty well-established churches in Russia. Besides

Russia, the Lord has been moving in other eastern European countries, such as Poland, Albania, Romania, and Armenia. This has been the Lord's doing. We have just followed His leading. Our going to Russia has been of the Lord's will for the accomplishment of His economy. This is the experience of having faith in God without doubting, and believing that we have received what we have asked for so that we receive it. We have to pray according to God's will for the fulfillment of His economy. Then we are one with God and the right persons in God's eyes. Then we have the assurance that we have received what we have prayed for.

The second testimony is concerning my experience of the Lord in 1943, which was a critical year of the war between China and Japan. I was very much oppressed by the military police of the Japanese invading army in my city. One night I had a dream in which the Lord assured me that I would not be harmed by them. In that dream I was walking and I came to a slope with four steps. After I stepped down, a German shepherd jumped up and put its front paws upon me, but the dog did not hurt me. When it stopped bothering me, I saw the day dawn, like the dawning in the morning, with a broad highway, very bright and very straight. After waking up, I realized that this was not an ordinary dream.

As I considered this dream, I received its interpretation. The four steps were the last four years of the war, which were very difficult in China. There were eight years of fighting between Japan and China, and the last four years, after America joined the war, became very hard. The Japanese military police arrested me, but before they did I had this dream. I realized that the German shepherd signified the Japanese who were troubling me but who eventually did not do any harm to me. After this troubling there was a broad highway shining under the dawning of the day. I then knew that after the Japanese trouble, the Lord would bring me onto such a highway.

I had this dream fifty-three years ago, when I was only thirty-nine years old, in 1943. After 1943, because of being imprisoned by the Japanese, I became sick with tuberculosis of the lungs. The doctor charged me to rest absolutely in bed for six months. In October 1944 I left Chefoo and rested in Tsingtao for another one and a half years until 1945 when the Japanese surrendered. After the war, the brothers in Shanghai and Nanking asked me to visit the churches. In 1948 the political situation changed in China, and Brother Nee made the decision to send me out. I went to Taiwan in 1949 to minister Christ for the establishing and building up of the churches there. Eventually, I came to the United States and began to minister here for the Lord's recovery in 1962. I never dreamed that I would be here. Today the whole earth is open to the recovery. During all my time in the church life, I have never seen such a harmony among the churches, among the elders, and among the co-workers as today. By His mercy and grace, we can boast that today on this whole earth, all the churches, the co-workers, and the elders are in harmony. Every sign is an encouragement. Every report is beautiful. The Lord is working everywhere. The open door to the Lord's recovery is His doing. For this move, I have prayed at rest, believing that I have what I have asked for.

If we ask the Lord for things that satisfy our desire, we will not receive anything. This is because our prayer is not according to God's will for the fulfillment of God's economy, and we are not the right persons. First, we must be the right persons, absolutely one with God. One night, during my imprisonment by the Japanese for thirty days, I looked up and said, "Lord, You know why I am here." At the time it seemed as if the Lord Jesus was right before me. I had the full assurance to say to the Lord, "Lord, I am imprisoned for Your sake." We must first be the right persons before God, persons who are one with God. Then we can have God as our faith and pray according to our knowledge of God's will for the fulfillment of His economy. If we pray for something according to our desire, not according to God's will, to fulfill our purpose, not to fulfill God's economy, we can never have the faith in God to believe that we have received what we asked for.

K. Teaching Them How to Flee by Prayer

In prophesying that the returned Israel in the future will suffer the great tribulation, the first God-man taught them how to flee by prayer (Matt. 24:15-22). According to God's economy, He gave up Israel but He would not give them up for eternity. This is a temporary matter. The Lord Jesus told the leaders of Israel in Matthew 21 that God would give them up. Then in Matthew 24 the Lord prophesied that the dispersed Israel would eventually return to their holy land. But at the end of this age, because of Antichrist, a great tribulation (Matt. 24:21) will occur in the holy land, so Israel will suffer. The Lord told them to pray, asking God to save them.

1. That Their Flight May Not Be in Winter nor on a Sabbath

The Lord told them to ask God that their flight would not be in winter nor on a Sabbath (Matt. 24:20). Winter is a time when escape is difficult. Also, on the Sabbath one was allowed to walk only a short distance (see Acts 1:12, note 2), a distance not adequate for escaping.

2. Believing That God Is in Control

They should believe that God is the One who controls the weather and the surrounding environment. To pray that they do not flee in winter is to ask God to control the weather. To pray that their flight is not on a Sabbath day is to ask God to manage their environment. When we ask God to do something, we must be the right persons, persons for God's economy on this earth. We must also be one with God so that we can believe that the very God to whom we pray controls the weather and rules the world situation.

L. His Prayer in Gethsemane

In His prayer in Gethsemane before He was arrested, judged, and sentenced to be crucified, He prayed and taught His disciples to learn from Him how to pray (Matt. 26:20-30, 36-46).

1. Teaching His Disciples How to Remember Him

After the Feast of the Passover, He taught His disciples how to remember Him by breaking the bread and drinking the cup (vv. 20, 26-29). He was firstly eating the Passover according to the Old Testament. Then at the end of that feast, He established the Lord's table to remember Him by breaking the bread and drinking the cup.

2. Burdened to Go to Gethsemane

He was burdened to go to Gethsemane, a quiet place, deep in the night, with His disciples, to pray (vv. 30, 36).

3. Being Sorrowful and Deeply Distressed

He took Peter, John, and James aside and began to be sorrowful and deeply distressed, saying to them, "My soul is exceedingly sorrowful, even to death," and asking them to remain there and watch with Him (vv. 37-38). He was sorrowful, even sweating with drops like blood (Luke 22:44), because He realized the full meaning of the great commission for Him to die for the accomplishment of God's redemption for God's fallen people. This burden was too great. We should not forget that He was a human. To be crucified on the cross was a real suffering. He also knew that Judas, the betrayer, would bring others to arrest Him. In His humanity He was exceedingly sorrowful, distressed even to death. He brought the disciples to the garden of Gethsemane to pray. When they arrived He took Peter, John, and James, these three intimate ones, aside. This shows that how far we can follow the Lord depends on our situation with Him. Then the Lord even left these three to pray.

He went forward a little, fell on His face, and prayed, saying, "My Father, if it is possible, let this cup pass from Me; yet not as I will, but as You will" (Matt. 26:39). *This cup* refers to His death on the cross. In His humanity He was so submissive in His suffering. In His humanity such suffering was nearly unbearable, yet He prayed for the Father's will, not His will, to be done. He went away a second time and prayed, saying, "My Father, if this cannot pass away unless I drink it, Your will be done" (v. 42). He left them and went away again and prayed a third time, saying the same word again (v. 44). Philippians 2 says that He was obedient even to death, and that the death of a cross (v. 8).

4. *Asking God to Save Him out of Death*

The first God-man's prayer here, like all His prayers in
the synoptic Gospels, was prayed by Him in His humanity;
this prayer here, made by Him when He was exceedingly
sorrowful and deeply distressed, corresponds with the one in
Paul's writing in Hebrews 5:7 in which He offered up both
petitions and supplications with strong crying and tears,
asking God to save Him out of death. He was praying under
this kind of condition, but He still was submissive and
obedient to the Father. We need to see that the Lord prayed
this way in His humanity, in which He was troubled. In
John 10 He is the good Shepherd who would lay down His
life for His sheep. He was willing to do that in His divinity.
But in His humanity, He was sorrowful.

5. *The Prayer in Gethsemane Being after His Prayer in John 17*

The Lord's prayer in Gethsemane was after Christ's
prayer in John 17 as the conclusion of His divine teaching
in John 14—16 concerning the union, mingling, and incorporation of the processed and consummated Triune God with
His chosen and redeemed people, which was prayed in Christ's
divinity. We have to make a distinction between Christ's
prayer in His humanity and His prayer in His divinity. All
the prayers in the first three Gospels were made by Christ
in His humanity. Only the prayers in John were made by
Christ in His divinity. This is because the first three Gospels
are related to Christ's humanity as the King, the Slave, and
the Man, but John is concerning Christ as God. Thus,
whatever He did in John was done by Him in His divinity.
In John the Lord said, "I and the Father are one" (10:30).
Such a word was not recorded in the first three Gospels.
Then He said that as the sent One, He was not alone, because
the Sender, His Father, was with Him all the time in His
divinity (16:32; 8:16, 29). We will cover the Lord's prayer in
John 17 in the Crystallization-study of the Gospel of John,
in the upcoming summer training.

THE GOD-MAN LIVING

MESSAGE SEVENTEEN

THE FIRST GOD-MAN'S LIVING
A MAN OF PRAYER

(8)

Scripture Reading: Matt. 26:20-30, 36-46; Luke 23:33-34; Matt. 27:46; Luke 23:46

OUTLINE

II. The divine facts in the mystical human life of the first God-man in the record of the synoptic Gospels concerning the first God-man as the King-Savior in the kingdom of the heavens, the Slave-Savior in God's gospel service, and the Man-Savior in God's salvation:

L. In His prayer in Gethsemane before He was arrested, judged, and sentenced to be crucified, He prayed and taught His disciples to learn from Him how to pray—Matt. 26:20-30, 36-46:

6. He taught His disciples how to watch and pray:

a. He came to His disciples and found them sleeping. He said to Peter, "So were you not able to watch with Me for one hour? Watch and pray that you may not enter into temptation. The spirit is willing, but the flesh is weak"—vv. 40-41.

b. He came again and found the disciples sleeping, for their eyes were heavy—v. 43.

c. He came to the disciples the third time and said to them, "Are you still sleeping and resting? Behold, the hour has drawn near, and the Son of Man is being delivered up into the hands of sinners. Arise, let us be

going. Behold, the one who is betraying Me
has drawn near"—vv. 45-46:

  1) The Lord took Peter, John, and James,
who were more close and intimate to Him
(see Matt. 17:1), apart from the rest of
the disciples particularly and charged
them to watch with Him—vv. 37-38.

  2) They did not keep the Lord's word,
because they were weak in their flesh
even though they were willing in their
spirit—vv. 40-41.

  3) This shows us the reason that we do not
watch with the Lord in our prayer.

M. On the cross Christ prayed three times:

  1. The first time, He prayed for those who were
crucifying Him—Luke 23:33-34:

    a. This was prophesied by Isaiah (53:12).

    b. This indicates that the first God-man as a
genuine man did have a spirit to forgive His
opposers according to what He taught us to
pray in Matthew 6:12, 14-15.

    c. He did this in His humanity with the divine
power of the eternal Spirit—Heb. 9:14.

  2. The second time, He prayed to God, saying, "My
God, My God, why have You forsaken Me?"—
Matt. 27:46:

    a. Christ's crucifixion lasted for six hours from
9:00 A.M. to 3:00 P.M. (Mark 15:25; Matt.
27:45). In the first three hours He was
persecuted by men for doing God's will; in
the last three hours He was judged by God
for our sins (1 Cor. 15:3).

    b. In the last three hours of His crucifixion
God had caused our iniquity to fall on Him
(Isa. 53:6) and made Him sin for us (2 Cor.
5:21), so God left Him at that juncture.

    c. Christ's prayer here seems to contradict His
word that God the Father was with Him

while He was on the earth (John 8:16, 29;
16:32).

d. This is due to the different views of the
synoptic Gospels and the Gospel of John.
The view of the synoptic Gospels is physical
concerning Christ in His flesh, that is, in
His humanity; whereas the view of the
Gospel of John is mystical concerning Christ
in His divinity.

e. According to John's record in the mystical
view concerning Christ in His divinity, God
the Father with Him and the Spirit as the
Triune God are always one essentially,
coexisting and even coinhering; this is what
is called the essential Trinity; whereas
according to the record of the synoptic
Gospels in the physical view concerning
Christ in His humanity, God the Father left
Him economically when He was made sin
for us on the cross; this is what is called
the economical Trinity.

f. First Peter 3:18 unveils to us that when
Christ suffered for our sins, on the one hand,
He was crucified in His flesh (in His
humanity), but on the other hand, He was
made alive in the Spirit (in His divinity).
This proves that concerning Christ there are
two different views: the first one according
to His humanity and the second one according to His divinity.

g. He cast out demons in His humanity by the
Spirit of God (Matt. 12:28), and He performed the miracles of feeding the five
thousand and feeding the four thousand in
His humanity by the blessing of the Father;
all these prove that what Christ did in the
synoptic Gospels was in His humanity with
His divinity.

h. It is in His humanity that He prayed to the

Father with sorrow and distress (Matt.
26:37-38), sweating with drops like blood
(Luke 22:44), and even cried strongly with
tears, asking God to save Him out of death
(Heb. 5:7). At that juncture, He needed an
angel to strengthen Him (Luke 22:43), needless to say that He needed the Spirit to
support Him (Heb. 9:14).

3. The third time, He cried with a loud voice,
before He expired, saying, "Father, into Your
hands I commit My spirit"—Luke 23:46:

a. This tells us that the first God-man as a
genuine man trusted in God to the end of
His human life.

b. Surely such a prayer of Christ was made
by Him in His humanity.

Many readers of the Bible feel that in studying the four Gospels, the easiest thing to study is Christ's prayer. This concept is wrong. The prayers in Matthew, as we have seen, are hard to understand. They show us how to pray according to God's will for the accomplishment of God's economy.

In this message we will conclude our fellowship concerning the God-man living, specifically concerning Christ as a man of prayer. Among other things, we want to consider the Lord's prayer on the cross in which He said, "My God, My God, why have You forsaken Me?" (Matt. 27:46). It is difficult to reconcile this portion of the Word with what the Lord said in John concerning God the Father's always being with Him as God's sent One (16:32; 8:16, 29). God the Father was with Him all the time, but when He was dying on the cross, He cried, "My God, My God, why have You forsaken Me?" We need to see how to reconcile these two portions of the Word.

We want to emphasize that we are still fellowshipping concerning the divine facts in the mystical human life of the first God-man. The significance of the loaf on the Lord's table has two aspects. One is the physical aspect, and the other is the mystical aspect. The loaf, on the one hand, signifies the Lord's physical human body of blood and flesh, which He gave for us on the cross in dying for us and for our sins. At the same time, that loaf signifies Christ's mystical Body. The physical body is judicial. The mystical Body is organic. We are the mystical Body of Christ. We have been baptized in one Spirit into this one Body (1 Cor. 12:13), and God has placed us and blended us together in this one mystical Body (vv. 18, 24).

Such a mystical view can be possessed only by the seeking Christians. Like the Lord Jesus, we need to be those who are apparently physical, yet invisibly mystical. All the genuine prayers, real prayers, prayers that can be counted by God, are divine facts in the mystical human life. We have seen that before the Lord fed the five thousand, He prayed by looking unto His Father (Matt. 14:19). This is something divine, performed in a mystical human life.

6. *Teaching His Disciples How to Watch and Pray*

Now we want to conclude our fellowship from the previous message concerning the Lord's prayer in Gethsemane, where He taught His disciples to learn from Him how to pray (Matt. 26:20-30, 36-46).

a. *The Spirit Being Willing but the Flesh Being Weak*

In Gethsemane the Lord came to His disciples and found them sleeping. He said to Peter, "So were you not able to watch with Me for one hour? Watch and pray that you may not enter into temptation. The spirit is willing, but the flesh is weak" (vv. 40-41). Watching and praying is a very strong principle in our Christian life because the tempter, Satan, is always around us. The more we love the Lord, the more the tempter pays attention to us. Once we turn to the Lord to love Him, Satan would not stop trying to trouble us. There is a battle and a struggle in this universe between God and Satan.

I believe that the Lord's telling His disciples to watch and pray was also His warning to Peter. Eventually, Peter entered into Satan's temptation in the same night. He denied the Lord to the Lord's face three times. Surely he was not watching and praying at that time. In the same night, Peter entered into temptation due to his not watching and praying.

There is another principle of the seeking believers of Christ. This principle is that all the time their spirit is willing, but their flesh is weak. This is a principle not only in prayer but also in the entirety of the Christ-seeking life. Our spirit desires to be an overcomer, but our flesh is weak. We have the desire in our spirit, but we do not have the strength in our flesh. This is why we should not trust in the flesh but take care of our spirit.

b. *Finding the Disciples Sleeping*

When the Lord came again to the disciples, He found them sleeping, for their eyes were heavy (v. 43).

c. The Reason We Do Not Watch with the Lord in Prayer

The Lord came to the disciples the third time and said to them, "Are you still sleeping and resting? Behold, the hour has drawn near, and the Son of Man is being delivered up into the hands of sinners. Arise, let us be going. Behold, the one who is betraying Me has drawn near" (vv. 45-46). While the disciples were sleeping, the Lord was fighting in His prayer, even to the extent of sweating with drops like blood (Luke 22:44).

The Lord took Peter, John, and James, who were more close and intimate to Him (see Matt. 17:1), apart from the rest of the disciples particularly and charged them to watch with Him (26:37-38). They did not keep the Lord's word, because they were weak in their flesh even though they were willing in their spirit (vv. 40-41). This shows us the reason that we do not watch with the Lord in our prayer. Our spirit is willing, but we have a problem with our flesh, which includes our self.

M. Christ Praying Three Times on the Cross

1. Praying for Those Who Were Crucifying Him

On the cross Christ prayed three times. The first time, He prayed for those who were crucifying Him (Luke 23:33-34). While the persecutors were crucifying Him, He asked the Father to forgive them because they did not know what they were doing. This was prophesied by Isaiah (53:12). This indicates that the first God-man as a genuine man did have a spirit to forgive His opposers according to what He taught us to pray in Matthew 6:12, 14-15. The Lord taught that if we do not forgive our debtors, this will annul our prayer. To have our prayer answered, we must forgive those who are indebted to us.

Christ prayed, asking the Father to forgive those people who were crucifying Him, in His humanity with the divine power of the eternal Spirit. Hebrews 9:14 says that He offered Himself to God by the eternal Spirit. For Him, as also a human being, to be offered to God as a burnt offering and as a sin offering on the cross was not an easy thing, so He needed the eternal Spirit to sustain Him. To pray for the forgiveness of those who were crucifying Him was not an easy thing, but He did it in His humanity with the divine power. This is a divine fact performed in a human life—yet not the physical human life, but the mystical human life—by the divine power of the eternal Spirit.

2. Praying, "My God, My God, Why Have You Forsaken Me?"

The second time, He prayed to God, saying, "My God, My God, why have You forsaken Me?" (Matt. 27:46).

a. Persecuted by Men and Judged by God

Christ's crucifixion lasted for six hours from 9:00 A.M. to 3:00 P.M. (Mark 15:25; Matt. 27:45). In the first three hours He was persecuted by men for doing God's will; in the last three hours He was judged by God for our sins (1 Cor. 15:3).

b. Causing Our Iniquity to Fall on Him

In the last three hours of His crucifixion God had caused our iniquity to fall on Him (Isa. 53:6). Very few Bible students have seen these two sections of time. Man's persecuting, crucifying, mocking, and despising were in the first three hours from 9:00 A.M. to noon. Then at noon the whole universe became dark because at that time God was judging Christ because of our sins. The Bible tells us He bore our sins, because God cast that burden upon Him. God caused our iniquity to fall on Him and even made Him sin for us (2 Cor. 5:21), so God left Him at that juncture. At that time He became the unique sinner in the universe. He was even the totality of sin. God made Him sin for us, yet He Himself did not sin. Even He did not know what sin was.

c. Christ's Prayer Here Seeming to Contradict His Word That God the Father Was with Him

Christ's prayer here seems to contradict His word that God the Father was with Him while He was on the earth (John 8:16, 29; 16:32).

d. Due to the Different Views of the Synoptic Gospels and the Gospel of John

This is due to the different views of the synoptic Gospels and the Gospel of John. The view of the synoptic Gospels is physical concerning Christ in His flesh, that is, in His humanity. The first three Gospels—Matthew, Mark, and Luke—were written with the physical view concerning Christ in His humanity as a King in Matthew, a Slave in Mark, and a human Savior in Luke. But the view of the Gospel of John is mystical concerning Christ in His divinity. Only the Gospel of John is written with the view of Christ being God.

e. The Essential and Economical Aspects of the Trinity

According to John's record in the mystical view concerning Christ in His divinity, God the Father with Him and the Spirit as the Triune God are always one essentially, coexisting and even coinhering. To coinhere is to mutually indwell one another. The three of the Godhead are coinhering, mingled, and blended as one. This is what is called the essential Trinity. But according to the record of the synoptic Gospels in the physical view concerning Christ in His humanity, God the Father left Him economically when He was made sin for us on the cross; this is what is called the economical Trinity.

The essential Trinity is according to God's essence. The economical Trinity is according to God's move. John 14 says that the Father is in the Son and the Son is in the Father. They two are one. Eventually, They work to bring us into Them, that is, into the union, mingling, and incorporation with the Triune God. John reveals that we have been united with, mingled with, and even incorporated into the Triune God. But in Matthew and Luke, the synoptic Gospels, when Christ was being baptized, He stood in the water on earth praying. At that juncture, God the Father spoke from heaven, and God the Spirit was soaring in the air (Matt. 3:16-17; Luke 3:21-22). The three of the Divine Trinity were in three different locations. The Father was in heaven; the Son was on the earth; and the Spirit was soaring in the air. Even though They were separated economically, They were still one essentially.

f. Crucified in the Flesh and Made Alive in the Spirit

First Peter 3:18 unveils to us that when Christ suffered for our sins, on the one hand, He was crucified in His flesh (in His humanity), but on the other hand, He was made alive in the Spirit (in His divinity). This proves that concerning Christ there are two different views: the first one according to His humanity and the second one according to His divinity. Christ is both God and man, possessing the divine nature, divinity, and the human nature, humanity. When He was crucified to death, He did not die in His divinity, but He was killed in His humanity for our sins. In the meantime He was working in His divinity. In the physical view of Christ in His humanity, He was killed. In the mystical view of Christ in His divinity, He was empowered with life.

g. What Christ Did in the Synoptic Gospels Being in His Humanity with His Divinity

He cast out demons in His humanity by the Spirit of God (Matt. 12:28), and He performed the miracles of feeding the five thousand and feeding the four thousand in His humanity by the blessing of the Father; all these prove that what Christ did in the synoptic Gospels was in His humanity with His divinity.

h. Praying in His Humanity and Needing the Spirit to Support Him and Even an Angel to Strengthen Him

It was in His humanity that He prayed to the Father with sorrow and distress (Matt. 26:37-38), sweating with drops like blood (Luke 22:44), and even cried strongly with tears, asking God to save Him out of death (Heb. 5:7). At that juncture, He needed an angel to strengthen Him (Luke 22:43), needless to say that He needed the Spirit to support Him (Heb. 9:14). As a man He offered Himself in His humanity to God, so He needed the eternal Spirit to support Him.

3. Committing His Spirit into the Father's Hands

The third time, He cried with a loud voice, before He

expired, saying, "Father, into Your hands I commit My spirit" (Luke 23:46). This tells us that the first God-man as a genuine man trusted in God to the end of His human life. Surely such a prayer of Christ was made by Him in His humanity.

We need to see that the prayers made by Christ in the synoptic Gospels were made by Him in His humanity with His divinity. But His prayer in John 17 was not in His humanity but in His divinity. John 17 shows us how Christ prayed that His believers would practice the oneness of the Divine Trinity as the Divine Trinity does. He prayed that the Father would make us one as He and the Father are one. We are to be one in Them as They are one (vv. 21-23). This is the oneness of the Triune God. We cannot practice this oneness in ourselves. We must practice it in the Triune God and according to what the Triune God does.